Stay Tru

How To Be Competitive In Today's Society Without Compromising Your Beliefs

For Young Adults, Athletes,
Parents, and Mentors.
The crossover from competition to
life and how it affects your faith.

Michael Magee III

Visit www.staytrulife.com
Stay Tru logo is a trademark of Yak Yak Life LLC

Stay Tru: How To Be Competitive In Today's Society Without Compromising Your Beliefs

Copyright 2013 by Michael Magee III. All rights reserved
Cover Artwork: Troy Lefevra
Designed by: Troy Lefevra

Published by Yak Yak Life LLC
All scripture quotations, unless otherwise indicated, are taken from the Holy Bible, New International Version®, NIV®. Copyright ©1973, 1978, 1984, 2011 by Biblica, Inc.™ Used by permission of Zondervan. All rights reserved worldwide. www.zondervan.com The "NIV" and "New International Version" are trademarks registered in the United States Patent and Trademark Office by Biblica, Inc.™

Dedication/Introduction…

As we live life, sometimes tragic events happen that make us realize how precious time truly is. I lost my sister a few years ago and from that moment on I felt an urgency to give back and help individuals as so many have helped me. I had ideas of what I wanted to do, but sometimes it takes certain people to enter into your life to give you that extra push and confidence to make your thoughts turn into reality.

I have so many people that I should thank, but I want to keep this as simple as possible. The idea for this book has been in my mind for years, but it was a March evening, in a strip mall parking lot, where the idea started to develop into a real mission. I can't lie and tell you that it has been easy, as during the process of writing this book my life has had some amazing highs and some unfortunate lows. No matter what though, I owe a lot of this book to J.T. I appreciate the support, and how you brought so many things to light that I needed to change in my life in an attempt to truly live a Stay Tru Lifestyle, not through my words but through my actions. Words of appreciation are not enough, but I hope you realize how thankful I truly am.

To Big Dave and his family. When I was struggling to find the motivation to move forward, and finish what I had started, you came into my life and gave me hope. Your kindness to me has not been necessary, but still you choose to make me feel a part of your family. Your goals will be reached because if anyone is deserving, it is you.
Lastly…To my family –

Dad and Mom: Your lives have been an example of faith, love and moral character in both word and deed. Beyond that, your unwavering support of all my endeavors over the years is appreciated more than you know. I'm proud to be your son.

Matt and Josh: The older we get, our age differences matter less and less. It is just us now, and Sarah's passing has strengthened our bond. I'm happy to say we are more than brothers; we are friends. In this next phase I hope we continue to play the game of life, through our faith, as relentlessly as we did on the athletic field of competition.

My daughter Shaylon : You are a beautiful girl with a heart for Jesus. Stay Tru. I love you always.

My nephew and niece, Gavin and Payton (Sarah's children): You are a joy to all of us. When you smile, I see your Mom, and that makes me smile. I love you both.

As I said that day while giving Sarah's eulogy, "I know for my parents and surviving grandmother, who nicknamed her Pooh from the moment she arrived, it is truly difficult to let your baby go, but yet a comfort to lay her in the peaceful arms of Christ after so many turbulent years. We believe that is where she abides now, that her profession of faith was real even though in her human nature she was not strong enough to allow him to fight and win the earthly battles for her. The last battle has been fought and she has been found to be victorious through the blood of Christ." Everything that Stay Tru does is for Sarah. Her spirit lives on.

Contents

Introduction

One	Stay Tru	**1**
Two	Competitiveness….Do We All Have It?	**9**
Three	Using Your Competitiveness…The Right Way	**21**
Four	Wanting To Go To Heaven But Not Wanting To Die	**37**
Five	Failure is a Good Thing!	**55**
Six	What is Success?	**71**
Seven	Dare to be Different	**85**
Eight	Passion	**101**
Nine	Believe in Yourself…The Three S's	**115**
Ten	Become a Playmaker	**129**
Eleven	Top 1%	**141**
Twelve	Finish the Game Strong	**159**

Forward

The challenges of life today are overwhelming and very few people are prepared to face these challenges, let alone succeed. This is especially true for young men and women who are trying to prepare themselves for the rest of their lives. I found that Stay Tru is a book that presents many of life's issues and how to work through them because it is a book on real life issues that confronted the author.

I chose to enter the coaching profession because of my love for sports, my family background and because of the enjoyment of my sports family, my team mates. My parents were extremely supportive of my sports interests but also imbued the harmony of faith, family and academics. Of course, the challenges of hitting the curve ball accelerated my decision to focus on the ultimate team sport, football.

As a husband, father and college football coach for over 25 years with 12 years as a Head Football Coach, I have witnessed and continue to witness the endless stream of challenges that not only hit me between the eyes, but also everyone around me including coaches, players and staff members. Shelley and I dedicated our lives to working with our 3 children but also to all of the young student athletes that we recruited and coached and mentored over the years. College football is an extremely competitive world which now plays on large national stages with every action being dissected by millions everywhere.

Michael hits upon many of these competitive challenges in this book. A man I met years ago, he has a solid foundation of faith, character and belief that has allowed him to live and see how competitive life is and how to meet the challenges and impact the lives of others in a positive manner. After reading his book, Stay Tru, I plan to put it into my toolbox to help me better meet the competitive challenges of life today.

Urban Meyer
Head Football Coach
The Ohio State University

*The views and opinions expressed in this book forward are my personal views and are not an endorsement of this book and do not reflect the views and opinions of The Ohio State University.

Chapter 1

"Stay Tru"

On a sleepy August evening in 2011, a single knock at the front door changed my life. I was at my parents' house visiting with my father, when we heard the knock. I opened the door and saw a police officer standing there. He had come to inform our family that my sister had died. My beautiful sister Sarah, just 33 years old, my younger sister who I'd played with and fought with as a child – was gone. In the time it takes to hear one sentence, the life of our entire family – and my life – had changed irrevocably. From that moment on, I started to think about life differently. I started to look at my life and search for answers to questions I had never considered before.

I am Michael, and I work with athletes. Through my work I have had the opportunity to meet athletes and coaches at all levels. I have run youth athletic camps and have played pick-up basketball games with NBA and other professional players. I have stood on the driving range next to some of the best golfers in the world, watching them hit perfect golf shots with effortless grace. And I have had the opportunity to have meaningful, thought provoking conversations with college coaches at every level.

All these experiences have been amazing privileges for me. But when my sister died, I knew there was something that I was missing. Until then, my whole life had been focused on sports and competition, and that was enough for me. But now I realized that there was a void in my life, and I knew that I could do more - if only I could pinpoint what that was.

When I was growing up, athletics were a big part of my life. I came from an athletic family, and my parents were young, so as I was growing up my extended family was in their athletic prime. I quickly took note. I played many sports as a youth, but basketball was the sport I loved and found myself playing the most. I had a decent career playing in high school and at the small college level. I probably thought I was better than I actually was, but if I didn't believe in myself then who else would…right? Growing up, my friends and I would play or shoot hoops on a regular basis, always competing and trying to outdo the other. It didn't matter if it was a game of one-on-one or just a friendly game of horse, one thing remained consistent: there was no friendliness about it and everyone wanted to win at all costs. When you are a kid, bragging rights are like gold. The more you had, the better off you were. Looking back, I see that it was in those times, outside on summer days with friends and family, where my competitive spirit was born.

After my sister died, and I started to ask questions and reflect on my life, the memories I kept coming back to were those of happy summer days playing football with friends at the park or basketball with family members in the driveway. I thought about my parents and their sacrifice of driving us kids all over the place for practices and tournaments. Then my thoughts went to my sister, her competitive spirit and personality.

My sister was an athlete, and a good one at that. Some would say that she was the best athlete in the household, and mind you that my two brothers and I all went on to play a college sport, so that would be very high praise. When I look back, what others say may be right.

I gave the eulogy at her funeral, and here is some of what I said: "Sarah was always full of surprises. But, I think the biggest surprise to us all was when we found out that she was actually an athlete, and a good one at that. Up until her high school days she messed around and played sports, maybe in a Gus Macker basketball tournament or two, but not because she loved basketball, rather because she said "Gus Macker is great, a lot of cute guys walking around without their shirts on." However her freshman year she went out for the basketball team, made it and was the starting point guard. No small feat for a girl that never touched a basketball and would never consider actually practicing. Then she announced that she was going to go out for our high schools award winning Pom Pon team. Sarah had never danced a day in her life but had that family blood that made you feisty and always right in your own mind, yet I can pretty much guarantee didn't come with any good dancing genes. If you have ever been to a family wedding, you know what I am talking about. But with my mother's support and her brother's skepticism she not only made the team but lettered as a freshman and would for all four years of her high school career."

It was in those moments, when I looked back, that I realized my childhood memories, and our family's competitive nature, could be used as a tool to impact people's lives in a positive way. My purpose of doing more was starting to become clearer.

Stay Tru

With thoughts racing through my mind, I started to look back on my athletic career. I began to wonder what impact I made on other people's lives, if any. I found myself in a humble place, wondering if I had done everything for my own benefit and satisfaction. The answers I came up with were scary. Looking back at those times in my life, I could not give a great answer to what I did or why. I could only come up with the following:

I just did what I felt I was supposed to do.
I just did what I was good at.
I just did what I got affirmation for doing.
I just did what I saw my family and friends do.

Now, obviously I did not do everything I saw others do. I had great parents and knew right from wrong, but when it came to everyday activities one thing remained constant: I did them because they just seemed normal for the surroundings I found myself in. If you are an adult, maybe you can look back at your youth and relate or maybe those traits still hold true today. If you are a parent, maybe you see those traits in your children. If you are married, maybe you see those traits in your spouse. If you are in your teen years or early adulthood, maybe these questions ring true.

I then started to think about the athletes I had the opportunity to be around, and the numerous athletes that I trained. Finally, I discovered what I had been missing and what I was trying to pinpoint. We have a major identity crisis taking place in society today. What we say is most important to us in life is what we spend the least amount of time doing or cultivating during the course of a day, week, month or year. After I came to that realization something clicked, and my purpose was born.

I started to study athletes' behaviors and began to notice the behavior patterns of parents and coaches as well. Through that process, I realized that competition surrounds us everywhere, and we are all competitive. I started seeing that when in competitive environments, what we believe and who we are gets thrown out the window and we change - often in negative ways. There are three questions that led me to write this book, and in the process became the fundamentals of my thoughts. Your answers to these three questions are what forms the foundation of your character and your actions, including how you act in competitive environments, no matter whether it is on the athletic field, in your home, at school, around friends or family, or at your place of work. The three questions are:

Why do you do what you do?
Who do you do it for?
What motivates you to do things?

Write the answers down on a sheet of paper and keep that paper in this book as a reference for later.

In order to lead a mindful life, we must identify why we choose to do things. Since we are covering the topic of who we are and competitiveness, I think it is important to find out why we are competitive and where it originates. For me, I was destined to be competitive, it was in my blood, it was all around me. Being competitive was a natural thing for me as it may be for you. Maybe you learned competitiveness in

other ways, or after reading this book you may realize that you are more competitive than you had thought. Whatever the case may be, we are setting out to discover how competitive we really are and how to make sure that our competitive style does not change what we strive to become.

Who and what you are now is not who or what you will become; you must have a plan outlining where you want to go.

Why did I start off explaining all of this to you? Well, for me it just seems natural because I have the same daily competitive struggles as every other person on this planet, if not more. Identifying how competitive we truly are is only the beginning. It is very important to realize how we react when in competitive environments. When I understood that, everything clicked. I realized that we need to Stay Tru to our beliefs no matter what environment we find ourselves in rather than letting competitive environments change who we are. You could say that not only was my purpose born, but so was the cause Stay Tru!

As I look back, I can't remember a time when I didn't have a competitive spirit. It was during those times in my life, during my innocent youth, that I actually made many mistakes pertaining to how and why I used my competitiveness. It wasn't my parents' fault; they always did their very best to teach us kids the importance of doing the right thing. My mother gave me a saying for Christmas once that read: "Go into the world and do well. But more importantly, go into the world and do good." Thanks mom. I should have listened to you more long ago!

No, it wasn't anyone's fault but my own. I had all the tools in front of me, I just chose to not read the directions. I chose to assemble my own life the way I saw fit. I didn't get into trouble as a kid and I do not think I was a difficult child; however, looking back I could have done so much more and so much better. Couldn't we all have done more and couldn't we all still strive to do better?

The words Stay Tru have a specific meaning. The words are a challenge to everyone reading this book to Stay Tru to your beliefs and not compromise. If I accomplish what I set out to do when I wrote this book then you will feel challenged to be a shining light when in competitive environments rather than a dark influence. It is not my goal to talk about the 6 laws of this or that, or say there are 8 rules you must follow in order to be a competitor and a person that stays true to themselves or their faith. I am simply setting out on a journey to talk about, bring awareness to, and create conversations about issues I see facing individuals and youth in today's society regarding a trait we all carry within ourselves. Whether you are in the office, a boardroom, at home with your family or on an athletic field of competition; competitive people surround us. We all have that trait inside of us, in some form. I truly believe that. I am no pastor or preacher, just a man that struggles with my everyday faith and trying to do good in the world. So dare I say this? If we were not born with some form of competitive nature then would there be no sin? I'll leave that up to the theologians to decide as we dive into competitiveness and how to make sure it does not compromise who we truly are.

Every day I see examples in athletic competition of the tug and struggle within our youth, their parents and individuals as a whole in today's society. We struggle with competitiveness; how to handle it and use it in positive ways as we try to keep our faith and remain true to who we really are. Competition can bring out the best and sometimes the worst in us no matter what the venue (home, office, church, athletics, etc.). Have you ever asked yourself why that is? Have you ever seen your son or daughter, friend, family member or yourself react a certain way in a competitive environment and ask yourself, "Why are they (or am I) acting that way?" "How can I help them (or myself) with that behavior?" If not, then I will say two things. Good for you, and please keep reading because one day you might ask yourself such questions.

Lastly, this book is my way of doing more. It is a way to make a difference and to make sure that my sister's passing was a moment where lives were turned around, despite sadness and grief, not destroyed or changed for the worse.

Chapter 2

Competitiveness...Do We All Have It?

I believe that **yes**, we all do have a competitive side to us. You may say that you have a brother, mother, friend or long lost relative who has no competitive qualities at all. My answer to that is you just have not seen or been around them when their competitive side has come out. Or they just haven't found the topic, job or pastime that triggers their passion yet.

My cousin, Logan, is about sixteen years younger than me. Logan has Asperger's Syndrome and was diagnosed at a very young age. Watching him grow up through the years, I never saw a mean or competitive bone in his body. I marveled at some of the things he was attracted to (collecting silver) and his dedication to those hobbies. This pleasant, quiet cousin of mine seemed to squash my theory that everyone has the "competitive gene". It seemed that the harder I would try to find it or pry it out of him, the more I failed. Then one summer day up on the shores of Lake Michigan, I was doing a whole lot of nothing when I heard something. I turned around and saw Logan standing on the end of the dock fishing, getting frustrated, speaking to himself and flashing looks of disgust. This I had to investigate! Could my theory be right after all? As I walked to the end of the dock I asked Logan what was wrong. He said something like "That man over there is catching all these fish and I can't catch a thing." I smiled and thought to myself, **now we're getting somewhere**.

I asked him a few probing questions, something along the lines of, "Why does it matter? You're just out here having fun; who cares how many fish you catch, right?" I do not remember his exact reply but I promise you it was bred from competitive nature. He wanted to catch more fish than the man on the next dock. He wanted to be a good fisherman. He definitely did not want to sit there just enjoying the nice summer day. He wanted to catch fish. Logan, like everyone else, has a competitive side to him; I just hadn't known what he was passionate about - what brought out his competitive juices. Two great things happened that day: Logan found a passion (and is still an avid fisherman to this day), and my theory was brought back to life.

Breaking Down Competitiveness

Have you ever been in an argument? Have you ever disagreed with someone's opinion and voiced it? Well, that is a sign of competitiveness. You argue or voice an opinion because you want someone to hear your thoughts or beliefs, and you want to be right or at least acknowledgement that you could be right, right? You would be amazed at how many competitive conversations take place in a day. If you don't believe me, I challenge you to take one day and be quiet. Do not engage in conversations where opinions are being expressed. Just sit back and listen to what people are talking about and where the words and thoughts come from. You will be as surprised as I was.

Before you take me up on my challenge, follow my logic here for a minute. Competitiveness is derived from a sense of pride. I know I'm treading on thin ice here because the Bible has many verses that talk about the downfall of a prideful nature within us.

Leviticus 26:19 "I will break down your stubborn pride and make the sky above you like iron and the ground beneath you like bronze."

Proverbs 11:2 "When pride comes then comes disgrace, but with humility comes wisdom."

Isaiah 2:11 "The eyes of the arrogant will be humbled and human pride brought low; the Lord alone will be exalted in that day."

I think we all have pride as human beings and have to be careful how that pride is used. When used in the right ways it can be a wonderful thing. When used incorrectly, it can produce a downward spiral in our growth as individuals and definitely a major roadblock for us spiritually. I do believe we can be proud of the good things that we do while making sure we are doing them with the right intentions in mind, giving the glory of our accomplishments to God, and thanking Him for giving us the opportunity to do such things. It is fulfilling to build others up, acknowledging their good deeds, making sure they realize how we notice their efforts and, in some cases, are humbled by them. What is important is that we understand how we can choose to change the way we react in competitive situations and make sure our pride is in check. I think the first step in making change is understanding our competitive traits. That is what this book sets out to do, to help us all understand why we are competitive and how we can use those traits for good.

Galatians 6:4 "Each one should test their own actions. Then they can take pride in themselves alone, without comparing themselves to someone else, for each one should carry their own load."

Pride in Athletics

I see it every day. Pride and competitive spirits are never on display more than in athletics. Look around and you will see fans wearing their favorite team colors or jersey, taking pride in the fact that everyone around knows whom they are rooting for or where their allegiance lies. You will see moms wearing pins with their child's picture. When kids come to practice or a workout, their parents will sit and watch them for two hours. (practice, let me remind you, not games or matches - but practice - for 2 hours). We see parents and fans screaming at the top of their lungs rooting for their child or team to win. We see examples of fans that have superstitions because they actually believe wearing their hat a certain way will help their team win. I personally know fans that would complain at the idea of driving three hours to go visit family, yet would have no problem driving three to five hours to go root on their favorite team. Why do we do such things? Because it makes us feel good. If our team wins or our child plays well and receives accolades, it makes us feel good. It fills us with joy and pride. I could go on and on, but I think you get the picture (my mom used to wear face paint… yea mom). Is all of this a bad thing? No. When used in the right context and in the right way, it can be a wonderful tool that brings families, friends and communities together like never before.

When I was a senior in high school, my basketball team was making a run through the state tournament. My high school had a history of putting great basketball teams on the floor, but for some reason we could never get over the hump and make it past the regional tournament. We could always win the district tournament, but never the regional tournament.

That senior year of mine, as we were making our run through the tournament, you could see the community come together as each game brought new fans and a new wave of support. It was exciting and nerve-wracking at the same time. We did not want to disappoint our growing fan base, and we loved how our families and community bonded as one to show their support and dedication as we tried to achieve that elusive regional championship. Whether we won or lost doesn't matter for sake of this story (but we won!); it's just an example of how athletics garnered a town pride and brought a community close together in a positive way. As I look back at that time in my life, my only regret is that I did not play for the right reasons. I gave no glory to anyone in the end. I just celebrated, felt pride within myself and definitely had haughty eyes.

> ***Proverbs 6:16-17 "There are six things the Lord hates, seven that are detestable to him: haughty eyes, a lying tongue, hands that shed innocent blood."***

One of the things I love about sports is that it can teach you valuable life lessons. I am going to go out on a limb here, but I believe we should all be competitive in some ways. Being competitive allows us to better ourselves. We should all want to improve certain areas of our life. If we are part of a team, we should want to help our teammates become better, which eventually affects us in positive ways. If we do not strive to improve ourselves and our talents, then what are we doing with the gifts God gave us? In life it rings true as well. If you are a teenager, you should want to learn, grow and become a better friend, son or daughter, athlete and follower of Christ. If you are a parent, you should strive to create a Godly home, to do your best to ensure a safe environment for your children, be a good provider and a great role model - someone your family looks up to and admires.

When used the right way, your competitive spirit can help others succeed, and that in itself is very rewarding. If you play an individual sport or work alone in your career, don't worry: using your gifts and talents along with hard work and dedication always brings benefits to others, and it can be equally if not more rewarding than being on a team. In conversations I have had with coaches, athletes, pastors and other role models, one thing became very clear: it's not wrong to be a competitor, it's only wrong when a competitive spirit is used for the wrong reasons. Those reasons may include selfish play for individual accolades, a constant need for the spotlight or selfish behavior in competitive environments for personal or team success. If you think about it a little bit, I am sure a few examples come to mind that you have lived through or witnessed.

The Bible has many references regarding competition (remember I am not a preacher nor pastor, just taking the advice from Lou Holtz when he said, "Do what is right. If you have any questions then get out your Bible.") Here are two…

> *1 Corinthians 9:24 "Do you not know that in a race all the runners run, but only one gets the prize? Run in such a way as to get the prize."*
>
> *2 Timothy 2:5 "Similarly, anyone who competes as an athlete does not receive the victor's crown except by competing according to the rules."*

Parents, Coaches, Mentors

Have you ever seen a parent trying to coach his or her child? Have you ever been to a youth sporting event and heard a parent yelling instructions to his or her child from the stands even though he/she knows that they can't be heard? Now, I am not talking about words of encouragement; I'm talking about words of direction. Well I have, on more occasions than I would have liked. I have a name for all of that direction that you hear: **white noise**. Why is there so much white noise surrounding our youth today? Is it because we adults are competitive and want our children to succeed in anything they do? We all want our kids to be successful, but sometimes we have to ask ourselves where the boundary is between wanting to help our kids be successful and just being pushy. Parents who want their children to be successful encourage, motivate and make decisions **with** the child, **not for** them. They help the child understand that competition is fun and playing sports is a process, not an end result of winning and losing. A pushy parent, on the other hand, does not allow democracy to take place. Instead he or she creates an environment of dictatorship. They may sign them up for activities without asking the child. They do not take into account what the child likes or dislikes; instead they rationalize that the child is not old enough to make his or her own decisions yet. A pushy parent holds onto results way too long and focuses more on the outcome of a competition rather than on the manner in which the competition took place. Every sport has pushy parents.

I work with a lot of junior tennis players who are developing their skills, trying to improve and play at the college level. I'll never forget the first time I traveled to a junior tennis tournament to watch one of my athletes compete. When I arrived I saw all these parents sitting in one section of the tennis facility while their children were warming up. Some parents were talking to one another, some were reading a book and some were just sitting, watching in silence. I remember thinking to myself that it seemed odd that all the parents appeared to be so disengaged but thought it just must be what the parents do before the matches started. Surely when the matches started they would start to pay attention, encourage their child and become more engaged. Well, I was completely wrong. The matches started, and the parent's demeanor stayed exactly the same. How could these parents who drove hours and hours to let their child compete read a book in the middle of a match? I had to know what was going on, so I searched out a few parents that I recognized and asked. The answer shocked me. Then again, maybe it didn't. I was told that due to the behavior of parents at tennis matches, which usually means negative reinforcement and constant coaching, rules had to be put into place that kept parents and spectators from saying a word during a match. Basically the rules said, ***thanks for bringing your kids to the tournament. You can leave now or stay at a distance and watch your child compete in silence***. Once I let the news digest, I started to think about how many other youth sports could benefit from such a rule. I started to recall the times I would be watching an event and hear a parent in the stands yell at their child instructions as if they were trying to control their movements with a joystick in some video game. Mind you that at the same time a coach is yelling out to the player, too. ***White Noise***, I always think to myself.

Let me ask all you parents, coaches and mentors this: Let's say you are driving down the road and realize you're a little lost. You see a gas station and decide to stop and ask for directions. You pull in and see a couple walking out of the gas station. So, you pull up and roll down your window and ask them if they know where your destination is. They say they do, and at the same time they both start telling you how to get to where you want to go. Their directions may be exactly the same, but they might be using different words or different reference points that you must look for in order to find the place you're searching for. Would that be confusing to you? Would it be easier if just one person explained how to get to where you want to go?

Why do we feel it necessary to coach our kids on a daily basis? I do know why we need to parent our kids on a daily basis, but that is a whole other book. I am talking here about extra-curricular activities. Why do we feel the need to be their parent, coach and motivator all at once? Why do we confuse them with constant white noise? Could it be our competitive nature coming out in those moments? Could it be that we remember what motivated us in our youth, so we assume our children will be motivated in the same ways? Is it that we see potential in our child so we have visions already developing of what they could be or could accomplish? I think all these explanations ring true in some sense. Which leads me to an important topic: realistic expectations.

In my time as an athlete, and seeing athletes compete, I've observed an interesting phenomenon - the kids that are the best athletes at the ages of 10-13 will not necessarily be the best athletes when they are 16-18. Kids develop and mature at different paces. I have seen kids peak at the age of 13. I have also seen kids who couldn't make a team at the age of 13 be the star of the team at age 17. So where is the delicate situation, you may ask? It lies in motivation and expectations. You have to motivate in different ways. We will cover that in chapter four.

We are all competitive. And as parents, we need to become aware of the environment we are creating. Maybe you feel comfortable with your competitiveness and feel your pride is in check but have a competitive child and could use guidance on how to deal with or create safe environments for him or her. Later in this book, I will help you identify how you can use your competitive spirit in positive ways and how you can create a safe environment for your child or children you work with.

Remember Logan? He is a competitor - for the right reasons. He has no personal agenda, no ill thoughts or feelings toward anyone. Logan just wants to be the best fisherman he can be. If Logan is out fishing and sees other fisherman catching fish around him, then he wants a little piece of that action for himself. I am starting to understand what makes Logan so special, and that leads us into our next chapter and an important concept: how to be competitive and use that quality in the right ways.

Tasks

1) Rate yourself as a competitor on a scale from 1-10.
2) List five things you are competitive or passionate about.
3) Of those five things you listed ask yourself if you let your competitiveness get out of hand and, if so, how?
4) If you are a youth competitor do you hear "white noise?" If so, how or where do you hear it the most?
5) If you are a parent are you guilty of creating "white noise?" If so, how or where do you create it the most?

Chapter 3

Using Your Competitive Nature... The Right Way

The spirit of competition has been around for a very long time. After all, the Bible makes reference to it! I think the biggest trend taking place in competition now, compared to long ago, is that in today's society we fall into the trap of idolizing false gods. Athletics is big business, and so are the athletes that play those sports. You can't go anywhere these days without hearing or seeing images of athletes. We are in awe of what they accomplish. Children want to be like their favorite athlete, wearing their shoes (I begged my parents for Jordans) and trying to mimic their game or copy their moves. We flock to stadiums to watch their talent and cheer them on. We buy their merchandise because we either want to wear what they are wearing or use it as a way to show we're a fan. No matter what the case, we have to be careful that we remain just a fan and do not cross the line into obsession. That may sound crazy to you, but I have seen numerous examples of people's days ruined because their team lost a close game, or lost to their biggest rival. I believe that when a contest of any sort affects our mood, behavior, and our overall life - then we have crossed that line and gone too far. Do you know what the funny thing about that is? There is a secret that people do not realize. A tough loss affects the fan a lot more than it does the athletes who were participating in that contest.

How To Care, Without Caring

Athletes that I have been fortunate to be around, that have made it to that highest levels (top college programs or the professional ranks), are wired a certain way. It's hard to explain, and I don't mean to confuse you, but basically they care without caring. I know that sounds like a contradiction, but let me try to explain.

An athlete that makes it to the highest level has been playing his or her sport for a very long time. He or she has played many games or matches and will play many, many more. When you get to that high a level, you have basically seen everything there is to see in your particular sport, so nothing really surprises you anymore. They have been through great wins, tough losses and the intense emotions of playing well or playing lousy. It's like anything in life; the more you are exposed to it, the more used to it you become. Well, they are used to it all. These particular athletes have a mindset that is opposite of the casual athlete, or mindset of most young athletes. **They know how to let go**. They know that a tough loss hurts, but they also know that they cannot sit around and feel sorry for themselves. They know that they are going to have to get up tomorrow and go back to practice and start preparing for their next opponent. Sure, they will take a loss hard and feel bad about it, and yes, they care if they win or lose. But here is the key. They understand that their life in the sport is a process, not an end. If they had let a loss affect them the way it affects some of us fans, or the way it affects our young athletes, then they would not have made it to the highest level. Emotionally they could not withstand the swings over a period of time. Do you know what happens to athletes that cannot let go or who care too much? They let it affect them mentally. They let doubt creep into their minds. They let it linger to the point where it affects them the next day or during their next game or match.

Maybe you have experienced this yourself or maybe you see it in your child. Have you ever been to a sporting event and seen someone make a mistake, then one mistake turns into two, and then three or four? Have you seen the opposite as well? A team or individual who technically should not win a game or match does because they can let go and play freely when their opponent cannot. When a team struggles to let go and mistakes start to pile up one after another, then they play tight. The ones that are successful have the ability to let go. Sure, they care if they win or lose, or if they make a mistake, but they don't think about the outcome. They are more worried about the here and now rather than the what-ifs (what if we win, what if I mess up, what if we lose).

This doesn't just apply to athletics. I see it in people when it comes to their jobs and hobbies. They get very attached to the outcome of a particular event and care so much that it paralyzes them, not physically but mentally. I see people's behaviors change to the point that they start doing things that are out of character. They may get upset, or they may cheat to get ahead. Whatever the change is, it usually is not pretty or admirable. Maybe you've seen it yourself.

There is one last thing I want to share regarding top-level athletes and how they care without really caring. Most of us would say that a game or match is won or lost on the day that it is played, and we would be correct - but only partly. Yes, that is the time when they have to go out and make it happen, but they also know that the majority of their work has already been done. They have already spent hours in the weight room, hours studying film and game plans. Their bodies are ready and so are their minds. They are ready to go out and do the best job they possibly can and have no regrets regarding the end outcome.

We "normal" individuals are the exact opposite. We have a lot of regrets. We play the "what if" game. We second guess ourselves and ask, "What if I had done this or done that?" We ask ourselves these questions not because we lost, but because deep down we probably know we could have done more beforehand. We could have worked harder and prepared better, we could have run one more sprint or not skipped that day in the weight room. We could have stayed and worked just a little longer instead of going out with our friends. There are so many "what if" scenarios that we become consumed by them. Maybe we do not immediately think it, but the pit in our stomach lets us know those thoughts are close by. My wish for you is that you live life with no regrets. Take a moment to reflect on things that are important to you. Whether it is a sport you play, your career, or your family, you have to put in the work and prepare for any situation that may arise. Do not find yourself playing the "what if" game, wishing you had done more or prepared more efficiently beforehand. Put in the work now, do not take days off, practice with a purpose and make sure you are prepared. The more you practice the more equipped you will be to face anything that comes your way.

When it comes to our life of faith, I am sure we could ask the same questions. Maybe we can take a cue from the top athletes when it comes to preparation. Maybe we can do all the work beforehand so that when the day finally comes and we are in the game of our lives with God we can look Him in the eye and say that we have no regrets. We can proudly confess that we did everything we possibly could to prepare for game day. We trained our mind, body and soul. We read the scouting report and are ready. Remember, it's a process, not an end.

Priorities

Before we really dive into how competitiveness can be used in the right way, we first have to make sure our priorities are in the right place. We need to get them in check. Let's do a little exercise. I am going to give you a list, ask you a few questions and then ask you to rank the list from top to bottom (most important to least important). Here we go:

The list:

Family
God and Faith
Sports or Athletics
School or Job
Keeping Up with Friends

Activity 1: Rank, in order of importance, what is most important to you as a person.

Activity 2: Rank, in order of importance, what is most important to your family.

Activity 3: Rank, in order, what topic consumes most of your time during an average day.

Activity 4: Rank, in order, what consumes most of your thoughts and attention during an average day?

I did this exercise with 50 athletes (young and old), coaches, parents of athletes and teachers. I will get to their answers in a moment, but first let's look at yours. I would guess that your rankings for activities number one and two are pretty similar. I would venture that what is important to you is also important to your family. I suspect that when you compare your answers from activities number one and two to activities number three and four you see a little disconnect. Am I close?

In the survey that I administered, the data showed overwhelmingly that what we find most important to us as a person and a family is often what we spend the least amount of time actually doing or focusing on. How do you improve at something? The short answer is by doing. The more you do something, the better at it you should become. If we all agree on that, then why aren't we spending more time doing what is most important to us?

I am not going to analyze your priorities, I just want to point out that as a competitor it is important that we are using our competitiveness in the right way, aimed at the right things. It doesn't make a lot of sense to have God as the number one thing that is most important to us when we spend the least amount of time every week working on that relationship. When I took my own survey and answered those questions, I found that God and my faith were at the bottom when I ranked my list of things that I spent the most time on during the course of a week, even though they are most important to me in life. Now that I have brought that to light, it is my goal to make a change and make sure that what I find most important to me in life is reflected in the time I devote to improving in those areas.

Using Competitiveness the Right Way

So how do we use sports and competitiveness the right way? How do we use traits that sometimes hinder us and turn them into positive influences for ourselves, our family and friends, teammates or co-workers? The answer has a few parts. We already addressed one part of the answer when we looked at our priorities and outlined what is important to us and what areas we should be spending time on making sure we improve. Another part of the answer lies in looking at the influence we can have, or the platform we have been blessed with, when our priorities are in check.

Platform

There was a movie that came out when I was growing up called "The Program." The movie is based on a college football program that had a few rough years and they were recruiting in an effort to get back to the top of the college football landscape. There was a line in the movie that has stuck with me ever since. In the scene, the head football coach is arguing with a professor about a player's grade or participation in class. The professor tries to make a point, saying that the school is a university for higher learning, not a football vocational school. The coach comes back and says something like "When was the last time 80,000 people showed up to watch a kid do a chemistry experiment?" Before you get upset, I think education is very important! But, I want to point out here that athletics does give us an unbelievable platform to

be a great example and affect so many lives in positive ways. At the time I heard that line in the movie I was young and naive. I used that quote to further justify why I was an athlete and why I wanted to be the best one I could be. It was cool and admired by many. Today I look at that phrase and realize how wrong I was. I wish I could have understood the deeper meaning: that if you play sports, then it is important to have your priorities in the right place because you have a great opportunity to use your competitiveness in such an amazing way. People are watching you. You have an opportunity to set an example by the way you conduct yourself and the manner in which you compete. Athletics has a built-in audience. The only other built-in audience I can think of that is comparable to athletics would be the movie industry, and sadly, there are very few films coming out of Hollywood, or actors, that proclaim Christian values. Realizing what an amazing platform we have, and how our participation in sports can affect people should be inspiring. When used properly, it should leave us in humble awe.

Nowadays children start playing sports as early as age three or four. No matter what age a competitor starts, there always is an audience. The community might not be buying tickets, but we can be assured that mothers and fathers, grandparents, other family members and friends are there watching and being supportive. Kids realize that. From the first time they lace up a pair of shoes and compete they realize they are performing in front of an audience. We have a responsibility to make sure that children understand how fortunate they are and the importance of using their platform in the most positive ways possible. It is equally important that parents understand that they are the catalyst in helping children realize how to behave and use their platform properly.

Using Your Platform

I am so proud of myself - or you could say I am very prideful right now. I made it 2 ½ chapters into this book without using any reference to Tim Tebow. You might not think that is such a great feat, but I would be quick to point out that when writing about being competitive and not losing sight of who you truly are then I think it is an amazing accomplishment. This entire book could be about the examples of Tim Tebow. OK…moving on…

Here are two questions for you:

Question: Who has more of an influence on Christianity, a football player or a pastor at a large, growing church?

Question: Who has more of a platform or influence on leaving an impression on people regarding Christianity, an athlete or a pastor at a large church?

I am not trying to downplay the role a pastor has; they are very critical in spreading the message and making positive influences on our lives, helping us along our spiritual journey. My pastor, Pastor Ron, has been a tremendous Christian mentor for me and this book would not be written if it were not for him and our conversations. I am only pointing out the irony in today's society. OK - I can't resist a Tim Tebow story.

I recently saw a video of Tim speaking at a university a few years ago. He talked about how during his junior season, playing football at the University of Florida, he started to wear Bible verses under his eyes. Athletes sometimes wear a black make-up substance under their eyes because it helps them see more clearly (light attracts to dark substances therefore the light is being directed at the black make-up under their eyes rather than in their eyes). Tim used that space under his eyes to write a Bible verse that was dear to him. During his junior season, the University of Florida played for and won the BCS (Bowl Championship Series) National Championship, an amazing feat, right? I do not think it was nearly as amazing as what I heard Tim say next in that video I watched. Tim said that in that national championship game he wore "John 3:16" under his eyes.

"For God so loved the world that he gave his one and only Son, that whoever believes in him shall not perish but have eternal life".

A few days after the national championship game he was informed that within 24 hours of him wearing that verse under his eyes 94 million people Googled the verse John 3:16. Tim joked on the video that he was asking himself how there were 94 million people in the world that didn't know the words from John 3:16, and he has a point, but in all seriousness 94 MILLION people…really?

So I go back to my two questions I asked you a minute ago. I am pretty sure that even the biggest churches out there never had 94 million people Google or look up a Bible verse that the pastor talked about on any particular Saturday night or Sunday morning. I'll go so far as to venture that if the most well-known pastor out there spent an entire year talking about a particular Bible verse they couldn't get 94 million people to look it up.

Tim used his platform, which was a football field that night, to spread a positive message. Tim is obviously a very competitive person. I do not think you play quarterback and lead your team to a national championship without being competitive. We can all take a page out of Tim's playbook and use our platforms to send positive messages and use our competitiveness in the right ways.

You might be saying to yourself; "Well, that is not a great example because I do not have nearly the platform that Tim did in order to spread a positive message." I am glad you are thinking that. Using a platform to be a positive influence is not a competition. We do not get extra credit points from God based on the number of people we influence. I don't believe God cares about the number, He only cares that we use the platforms He gave us with a good heart and good intentions in mind to impact others positively. We all have different platforms. My platform is the youth and adults I work out with each day. Your platform might be your place of work, where you go to school, the teams you're on or a group that you share a hobby with. Maybe your platform is your church or small group you are a part of. No matter what your platform, God put you there for a reason. If you have a heart for Christ then He expects you to use the situations you find yourself in to be a living example of what it means to be a follower of Him. Whether your platform is big or small, God is using you, and intends to continue using you. The key for us is to get out of our own way so that we can be used however He sees necessary. Too many times we fight it and do what we feel is necessary. There is a big difference between the two.

Parents

Parents have built-in platforms: their household and those

who dwell there. You may have other opportunities but your main platform is right there with you each and every day. We have talked extensively in this chapter about using competitiveness in the right ways to influence others positively. This message is never truer than in your household.

You may have a spouse and/or children who look to you every day for guidance and watch how you react to situations. The example you set by your actions in competitive situations is magnified and often repeated in future time. So, in knowing this, how do we make sure we set a good example for those watching us closely?

Well, Ephesians 6:4 might be a good start:

> *"Fathers do not exasperate your children, instead bring them up in the training and instruction of the Lord".*

My interpretation of that verse is: **Fathers and mothers, do not spend time getting on your children with things that are not important. Spend time making sure that they know what is most important and if you have any questions on what that is, then please get out the Bible and study it with them.**

Let me tell you a story. I want to preface this by saying that I have a terrific family and extended family that I admire greatly. We are not perfect, but what family is?

As I mentioned in chapter one, my younger sister passed away two years ago. It was a tough time for my family, and for the first time in my life I had to be the strong one. I was used to my parents always being there for us kids and taking the role of being strong, but in this situation it was different.

I was with my father at my family's home when we got word that my sister had died. My mother was out of town and one of my brothers lived in a different state, so I immediately had to step up and help my father. We had to phone them both and get them home as quickly as possible. Then we had to make calls to our extended family members and share the devastating news with them. I do not remember a whole lot from those few days, I just remember not getting very emotional because I had to be there for my parents. I had to help them make arrangements, contact friends and work on the eulogy that I would give at her funeral. I did my best, as did my brothers, and when it was all over I just remember having the emptiest feeling I have ever felt. It was almost like I kept asking myself "now what?" For days you are surrounded by people giving you condolences while you are staying busy making sure everything that needs to be done is done. Then when it is all over, you are alone. There is no more noise, no more people around; it is just you and your thoughts. Well, needless to say, I lost it. All my emotions came pouring out of me. I was all alone and didn't know what to do. I ended up going to speak to a trusted confidante about what I was going through. During that conversation she asked me about my family, how we reacted in times of crisis, and so on. My answers were all rave reviews of how great my family is, how tight we are and how we come together in times of crisis to help one another. Then she asked me who my spiritual advisor was within my family. I started talking about my mother; how I admire her faith and how she sets a great example. Before I could finish, she stopped me. Then she asked me the same question another way; she asked who in my family holds me accountable spiritually. As I sat there pondering that question in silence, she added more to the question: who in my tight knit family, a family of faith as I proclaimed, holds me accountable and makes sure that when I die I'm going to heaven? She wanted to know who in my family has given me the greatest gift you could possibly give another person, the gift of the knowledge of everlasting life. I was stunned and taken back. For all of the positive things that I said about my family, that is one question that I could not answer because the reality was there was no answer. I went to church growing up, knew right from wrong, but I never had a family member ask me if I had accepted Christ in my heart and if I served Him. I never had a family member make sure that if I died I was going to go to heaven.

I could continue to write about five rules you need to follow in order to be a parent that teaches their children how to be a good competitor, but instead I told you that story for one reason. It all starts with using your platform as a parent to make sure that your children know what is most important. From there, if their priorities are in the right place and they have their spiritual advisor in their corner, then how can they ever fail on the playing field of competition? There is one saying that I have heard a lot when it comes to athletes that are Christians, and it is one that I recommend you share repeatedly with your children. If they can understand and get to a point where, as Tim Tebow says, **they are not concerned about what their future holds because they know who holds their future**, then you have done an amazing job; keep up the good work! I truly believe that when we can get the youth of today to that point, then you will see an athlete and individual who cares, without really caring. When we have God in our corner and trust fully in Him, then competitive outcomes become secondary. "It's not whether you win or lose, it's how you play the game". Sure we care about winning and losing, but we also understand that there is a much bigger game being played; A game for our salvation and the salvation of others.

Tasks

1) Are you an athlete or competitor that cares too much or holds on too tight, and finds yourself too focused on the outcome rather than the process? If so, explain some examples of situations where that happened to you.
2) If you are a parent, do you see examples of your child or other children hanging on too tight and caring too much? If so, explain what you see and how that affects them.
3) If you answered yes to either question one or two then write a paragraph on steps you will take to make sure you do not hold on too tight and can care without caring too much.
4) List a few things that you are going to do to make sure you start spending time on what is most important to you if you feel you are not currently doing so.
5) List three areas of your life where you feel you have been blessed with a platform.
6) In a paragraph or two, write down how you are using those platforms.

Chapter 4

Wanting To Go To Heaven, But Not Wanting To Die

I have to admit I use this saying a lot, mainly because I see examples all too often of people who want to attain certain goals, but they do not want to do what is necessary in order to achieve them.

When I go into work, I know my day is going to be spent dealing with two types of people. The first type are the adults who are seeking motivation or guidance because they want to lose weight, stay fit or be challenged. The second type of individuals are the youth athletes that I train. The youth athletes all have goals ranging from playing on their high school teams to playing at the professional level. While this is a wide range of goals and expectations that I deal with on a daily basis, I strive to treat every individual the same, no matter their age, goals or potential to reach those goals. Seems pretty simple, right? Well, this is where the confusion begins (at least for me). The individuals I enjoy working with the most are the toughest to deal with. Can you guess what group that is? You guessed it; it's the younger athletes. You may think that wouldn't be true, but it is. You might assume that the athletes that have so much to still accomplish would be very motivated, but that is far from the case. Now don't get me wrong: many young adults are very hungry to succeed and achieve their goals. However, I believe that only a small percent knows what type of effort it actually takes to make their goals become reality. Only a small percent know they will have to die in order to get to heaven.

By throwing a statement like that out there, it is only fair to examine why I believe this to be the case. I have spent time observing young adults and their parents and have asked and answered certain questions over and over.

Question: Why do young adults struggle in knowing what it takes to accomplish their goals?

Many would answer that times are different and children growing up today have so many more distractions than ever before. That would be the easy answer. While I agree with this to a point, I think the answer goes much deeper and can be broken down into a few categories:

1. Time

Today a trend is taking place when it comes to our youth. Based on numerous conversations with coaches and athletes at many levels, I conclude that the problem is not the individual; the problem is culture and time. Youth nowadays have access to so many things and that makes it hard for them to remain focused for an extended period of time. When you take into account social media outlets such as Facebook, Twitter, Instagram, texting and other devices, then you can start to understand why it is becoming a blessing and a curse.

I will surrender the point that all these social media devices have a positive side. They make it easy to communicate (Ask yourself if you had Facebook, Twitter and a cell phone when you were in high school, would you have been grounded a lot more than you already were?). They make it easier to stay current and they keep us connected to our families and friends more efficiently if used properly.

But…how can you keep a kid's attention for an hour or two when during every break they are running to their bags to glance at their cell phones to see who texted them? And trust me, if they don't have a cell phone, one of their teammates or friends does and they are getting the latest information from them. The youth of today have so much information at their disposal that it makes it difficult to get them to narrow their vision and focus on a specific goal, even if it is one that they adamantly voiced as something they wanted to achieve no matter what it took. My job in dealing with younger athletes today is simple and difficult at the same time. It has two parts: the first is gathering and keeping their attention by making them realize why they are training with me; the second part is motivating them through encouragement.

Another factor that's time-related is extra-curricular activities. How would you like to fit these activities into a week's worth of time: school or job, practice, games or matches, workouts, youth-group or Bible study, homework, music lessons, driver's training and National Honor Society or any other organization you may be involved with. Sounds like a lot, and it is. Follow the Stay Tru logic for a moment. There are 24 hours in a day. Eight of those hours you are sleeping, so that leaves 16 hours. Let's say you are at a job or in school for another 7-8 hours. That leaves us with 8 or 9 hours. Out of those 8 to 9 hours, people will spend another 3 to 4 of them at a practice, rehearsal or workout and the round trip drive time. After all of that, we are left with 5 hours. Out of those 5 hours, we need to fit in eating, homework, and other activities we are involved in such as youth group, Bible study, etc. Oh, and then there's our social life (I dare you to keep track for two days how much time you spend talking on your phone, texting or using technology in some way – not to mention actually spending time with another person). If you follow along, you will see that we are squeezing dry every ounce of time that we possibly can. If all this rings true, then when are we supposed to find time to work on the things that are so important to us?

Do you now see how our priorities have the potential to get out of whack? Our mindset is to commit to our extra-curricular activities and then try to find time for what is important to us rather than filling our calendars with what we have said are our priorities and then working in the extras. It is time to change that trend.

2. Hunger

We live in a society where we judge individuals on potential just as much as we do on results. Take professional sports, for example. If you watch any professional sports draft you will continually see athletes being drafted and paid millions of dollars on potential rather than on a body of work. Teams are always drafting on what they think will happen, not what they know will happen. Young athletes growing up are smart, bright and aware of this. It is a culture we think is reserved just for the top-level athletes, but we are wrong. That culture is being created everywhere; sometimes we do not even realize it.

I had a conversation with a parent of a very good tennis player not so long ago. We will call that player Sarah. Our talk was focused on Sarah's development and future workout schedule. During that conversation, after about 15 minutes or so, it struck me that we were not trying to figure out Sarah's future workout plans; we were discussing how we could motivate Sarah so that she would see the benefit of working out. It was an "*aha*" moment for me. It hit me like a ton of bricks in the forehead. After I realized what we were really talking about, my mind wandered and I began to feel bad, like really bad. I realized that I was part of the problem. Sarah was a very good tennis player, one of the best in the area. She knew that, I knew that and others knew that. I also knew that people kept telling her how good she was, patting her on the back, looking up to her and almost congratulating her for things she had not even accomplished yet, such as playing college tennis or dominating an upcoming high school tennis season. She was in a culture that I despise and, worst of all, I was in the center of it, being one of the main culprits. I was encouraging Sarah and making sure she felt good about herself and confident in her game. I was doing my job, right? Wrong!

Why would Sarah think she had to work out and continue to improve when she was constantly being recognized for what she was going to do rather than what she did do? Remember just a bit ago when I said my job consisted of gathering and keeping the athletes attention by making them realize why they are training and the second part being motivation through encouragement? Well, there is a fine line and I had to re-evaluate the line I was walking, as I am sure many of us do (read the solution in question 3 to see how I re-evaluated the fine line).

Question: Is it Their Fault?

There is no easy answer to this question. I am not trying to cop out, but my answer is ***yes and no***. Let's break it down into the "yes" and "no" categories.

Yes

Yes. I think it is partly their fault. Long ago I heard my grandfather say that the greatest gift that God gave us was the power to choose. (I think he heard it from his favorite football coach Lou Holtz). I have always believed that. We can give young athletes all the tools in the world to succeed, but in the end it is up to them to do everything they set out to do to the best of their ability.

Follow this example. I am not the world's best sports performance trainer or motivational speaker, not even close. Let me throw this at you. If the athletes I train win the majority of their games or matches that they play does that make me a better trainer than what my abilities allow me to be? Take the opposite approach, if most of the athletes that I train lose the majority of their matches or games that they play does that make me a worse trainer than my abilities allow me to be? I think that Tiger Woods, Michael Jordan, Peyton Manning and Roger Federer would find a way to be arguably the best athletes at their sports no matter who their trainer was (please know that Tiger Woods has won fourteen major championships with three different world class swing instructors). Their trainers or support staff help but they as individuals have the drive within to push themselves and become the best athletes that they could possibly be. That is their amazing trait. No one has to beg them to work hard or make sure that they show up every day to practice or their workouts. Granted, they may have their days that they just are not into it physically or mentally, but those days are few and far between. I have never worked out with a top-level athlete and heard excuses such as, "I cannot make it because I have a party to go to" or "I have friends that are coming over so let's skip today's session". When dealing with good athletes it is obvious that their motivation comes from within. At that point my job becomes simple, I just have to push them to give a little more than they are used to each day.

I could write a whole chapter on the excuses I've heard as to why certain athletes cannot make it to a workout or practice. Look at Sarah's story. My main job isn't pushing Sarah to give just a little more during our workouts than she is used to. My job with Sarah is to motivate her so that she shows up to the workouts. Once she is actually at the workout, then my job is to encourage her so that I can keep her focused for the full 45 minutes and then push her to give just a little more than she is used to. See the trends here?

Working out is just one aspect of a young athlete's performance. It is just a piece of the pie, as I try to explain to athletes and parents. If an individual's priorities are out of line and they struggle to have the self-discipline to work hard, to become the best that they can possibly be, then their odds of becoming successful in competition decrease substantially. I find this to be true with not just athletics but other areas of their lives as well. We can lead them to the water; we just cannot make them take a drink.

No

No, it is not their fault. Why? Because if I could write a whole chapter on the excuses I hear from young athletes, then I could definitely write a chapter on why they are allowed to get away with not showing up. I am not sure when the shift took place, but when I was a young athlete I didn't have a choice when it came to showing up or not. Granted, I had a choice when it came to the amount of effort that I gave or my attitude once I was there. But not showing up was never an option. I always showed up. My parents instilled into me that if I committed to something, then I had to see it through.

I used to get frustrated with the behaviors of certain young athletes and I couldn't figure out why they behaved the way they did. I couldn't figure out why they did not want to work hard or why keeping their focus was such a tough task. Did I have to change or did they? In pondering that question I tried to understand why they did what they did instead of trying to decide who had to change in order for us to get to some sort of level playing ground. Once I started to uncover why they acted a certain way, I was able to better understand the challenges that they face as young, growing athletes.

In question number one, I wrote about the "time" and "hunger" issues facing competitors today. Those issues are real obstacles that athletes must overcome. But why are they obstacles? They are obstacles because no one has taught young people how to turn them into strengths. Imagine the advantage that a young athlete could have over the competition if he or she knew how to solve the issues of time and hunger (passion, drive or fire). What would their potential be if they knew how to prioritize their lives, not obsess about the outcome and be able to focus and strive to accomplish what was important to them? I think their potential would be scary. Now, what if they were equipped with all of that knowledge *and* had a positive influence and role model in their life leading by example, clearing up all of the white noise that surrounds them? I think there would be no limit to what they could accomplish.

But until that happens, I have to conclude that it is not their fault. Athletes today do not know how to accomplish their goals. Unfortunately, for now there is too much white noise surrounding them.

The Parents

I cannot let the parents off the hook here either, although I am not pointing any fingers (trust me, I wouldn't do that). There is no other way to say this other than, well, kids are coddled a lot of times in today's society. I see example after example where our youth are put on pedestals for their potential rather than their accomplishments. I see examples of parents wanting success for their children more than the child does. If you don't want to take my word for it, just look in your next TV guide at all the reality shows that feature parents and their children in competitive environments. Now let me clarify, I am not implying that you as a parent reading this book fit that profile. But, I will go as far as to say that we all want our children to succeed and sometimes we can let our own personalities blind us about what message we are really sending our children and the youth who are watching us looking for our approval and our affirmation as adults.

Remember the story I told you in the previous chapter regarding the questions I was asked about whom in my family made sure I had received the greatest gift one could ever give? Let's say for a moment that in your home you

have done an amazing job, have said all the right things to your child and had all the important conversations. I hate to be a bearer of bad news here, but do you know what can diminish all of that good work in an instant? It is when your child sees you do the opposite of what you say. If you say one thing about competition and how to set an example in competitive environments, then you have to practice those same values that you are teaching. Youth today need to see consistency; they thrive on consistency. I would love to see a study on youths' moods and achievements when they have consistency in their lives compared to when they do not. I think the data would be overwhelming.

I have experienced this "do as I say, not as I do" mentality. I have seen parents who continuously say the right things and encourage in the right manner away from the field of competition but act totally differently once in the competitive arena. I went to a Baptist college, and I always had a hard time with those students who would be preaching to me Monday through Friday, only to see them worshiping something else on a Saturday night. It's kind of the same thing here. Do not be that parent that teaches all the right things and then yells at a coach for not playing your child. Try as hard as you can to be the same person in the stands and in the car after a contest as you are when you are at the dinner table or in their room having those great conversations. An example of a conversation that I hope to have with my kids one day would go like this... ***Do all things to the best of your ability and in the end, no matter what happens, give the glory to God and be thankful to Him that He has given you the opportunity to compete and be a positive influence through your actions while in competitive environments. Do not worry about the outcome and what the future holds because your future is*** *safe and secure. God loves you, I love you and it is for who you are, not what you accomplish.*

Question: What is the solution?

Remember the story I told you about Sarah, the junior tennis player? To refresh your memory, when I was talking to her parent about her schedule I found myself in a conversation that did not consist of her workout schedule but rather how to motivate her to make sure she worked out. I then went on to talk about how I was at fault for creating an environment of congratulating her on her accomplishments, sometimes before she even accomplished anything. I had to re-evaluate the line I was walking, and I did.

I broke down the environment into three segments, understanding, motivation and expectations.

Understanding

Look back at the three questions I asked you in chapter one:
Why do you do what you do?
Who do you do it for?
What motivates you to do things?

I asked the individuals I workout with these three questions and had them go home and think about their answers for a little bit and then write them down and bring them back to me. I knew that in order for me to properly and effectively do my job, I had to understand why they did what they did, who they did it for and what they felt motivated them to do more. Here are some of their answers.

Why do you do what you do? Some athletes play sports or compete because they truly do love it. Some do it because it's fun. Can you guess what the most overwhelming response was? Most play or compete because it's what their friends or family do, or did. It makes them feel like they are part of something larger than themselves and it makes others around them happy.

Who do you do it for? The majority of the kids gave one of two answers. Athletes play for themselves because they enjoy it, and the most popular response was because it makes them feel good to receive recognition from adults. Let me break this down a little. Young athletes love to receive affirmation from their parents, coaches, mentors or other adult figures in their lives because it makes them feel good. It makes them feel good when adults in their lives are happy with them. Ever notice when a child's mood seems eerily similar to your own? Youth love it when their mentors in life are happy. I know from my own experiences as an athlete that when I showed up to practice and my coaches were in a good mood, then so were most of us players. However when I showed up to practice and the coaches were in a bad mood, then it usually affected the entire team in a negative way.

What motivates you to do things? I ask this question to individuals I train because their answer is crucial to our relationship in working together. If I cannot properly motivate an individual, then he or she will have a very difficult time wanting to improve, or at least enjoy the process of improving. I usually get two answers. First, young athletes are motivated by recognition for their accomplishments and, secondly, they are competitive. Competitiveness in this context means that they do not want to be left behind.

Remember the answers young athletes gave when asked why they do what they do? One of the reasons they gave as to why they compete or participate is because they want to be involved in things that their friends or family are involved with. You can see that their answer to the last question shows their competitiveness coming out. If they are going to do something, then they do not want to be bad at it; they do not want to be left behind as others around them keep improving.

Let's wrap up this chapter with two main points that I had to re-learn in order to create a healthy environment that made young athletes want to improve.

Motivation

I used to think that I knew exactly how to motivate individuals. I thought that by pushing them when they needed to be pushed and praising them when they deserved to be praised was a perfect recipe for proper motivation. I have learned that I am not completely wrong; however, I am not completely right either.

Look back at the story of Sarah. I pushed her when she needed to be pushed and I praised her when I thought she deserved to be praised, but in the end that was not enough. What was I doing wrong? After sitting down with her and having numerous conversations, I started to understand what I was missing.

Have you ever watched someone close to you compete or do something that is important to him or her? Did you notice things that they may have done wrong as well as

notice many things they did right? Then, when it was all over and you had a chance to talk to them, did you tell them how great of a job they did, how great they looked out there and continue to build them up? I think we've all done that. I love praising people for the positive things they're accomplishing; it is one of the most fulfilling parts of my job. But the problem with that is this; I was not being totally honest with them. When I watched one of my athletes compete, I noticed the good and the bad, but I only focused on the good.

Sarah was stuck. She was not improving, yet everyone kept feeding her words of affirmation and building her up. In the process, nobody was pointing out things she was doing wrong, so she thought she must have been doing everything right. During one of our conversations she said to me something along the lines of "Why do I need to keep coming to workout? You keep telling me how great I'm doing and say that I'm going to play college tennis, so I just want to maintain that level." I couldn't believe what I was hearing. Worse than that, I could not believe that I had created a culture where one of my athletes thought it was okay just to maintain the status quo.

I explained to Sarah that in sports, as in life, you are either growing or you are dying. Nothing in life simply maintains. If something goes up, then at some point it is going to come back down. I told her that if she was trying to maintain, then she had already started declining. If you want to make sure you play college tennis, then you cannot maintain. You have to keep working to improve because if you're not, then someone out there who is working harder will take your spot.

After I drove that message home, I had to explain to her that she did not do everything right; that there were many mistakes or faults in her game that she could improve on to become better. I apologized for not pointing out those faults sooner. I re-evaluated my message and since then have had this conversation with every athlete I worked out with. Our relationships are much better now.

I learned that I could praise an individual while properly pointing out areas we could work on together to improve. I do not point out areas where they can improve and then leave them feeling like it's up to them to fix it; I let them know that we will fix it together. It is important to make sure individuals know they are not alone. They need to know they have your support and you are there to help them, through thick and thin.

Expectations

Once I figured out how to effectively motivate the athletes I worked with, I quickly learned that another piece of the puzzle was missing: expectations. I started to outline specific expectations that I had for them and the probable outcomes they could expect if they did not meet them. This process has been invaluable.

Once I was completely honest with Sarah and explained to her the consequences of not improving, things changed immediately. I no longer had to motivate her to work out. I actually had to do the opposite and explain to her the benefits of taking a few days off and resting. I think we all can learn a valuable lesson here.

When you are leading a household, a team or any individual, it is important that you lay out clear and specific expectations as well as the consequences of not meeting those expectations. It is equally important that you are completely honest in communicating when those individuals are not meeting those expectations before it is too late. What if I'd never pointed out where Sarah could improve and that led to her not receiving a college scholarship? If I had pointed those things out too late, whose fault would that have been? It would have been mine. I am her mentor and her trainer. I serve her, she doesn't serve me.

Let's look at this in everyday life. What if you saw a family member or friend doing something wrong but never said anything or pointed it out? Let's say that the things they were doing wrong led to them getting in trouble or falling short of accomplishing a goal. Would you feel partly responsible? Would you let your child get a math problem wrong because he or she got all the other ones right? Would you say that a 95% grade was good enough for them and they didn't need to know how to solve the problem they kept getting wrong because getting the majority of the problems right was good enough? I think you get my point.

With all of the things that were outlined in this chapter I hope a few things became clear. There are many reasons why individuals don't reach their goals. There may be a lot of white noise surrounding them or maybe they just don't know what steps to take. No matter what the reasons, one thing remains true. Showing up, hard work, dedication, attitude and holding yourself accountable doesn't take talent, it just takes an understanding of knowing that in order to get to heaven you will have to die. Hard work beats talent when talent doesn't work hard.

Tasks

1) Write down five goals.
2) Explain who, besides yourself, could help you accomplish your goals.
3) Set clear expectations and deadlines for your five goals.
4) Write a few paragraphs explaining how your life would be different when you finally achieve all of your goals, compared to now.
5) Share what you have written with someone that you would like to hold you accountable to achieve your goals.

Chapter 5

Failure is a good thing!

"The only things certain in life are death and taxes"
Benjamin Franklin

Have you heard that quote before? Believe it or not, I disagree with it to a certain extent. I think it should be expanded to: "There are three things guaranteed in this world, death, taxes and failure." We will all experience failure in our lives. You do not have to be an athlete or a competitor to experience failure; you just have to live. No one will ever go through life without sinning, correct? If that seems like an unfair example, then ask yourself if you believe anyone will go through life and succeed at everything they do. Will they succeed at all of their dating relationships, have a perfect marriage, friendships, parenting skills and careers? The answer is obviously no. So, we must learn how to deal with failure and use it to our advantage, so that we may continue to grow and have purpose in life.

When failure arises, people handle it in one of two ways. And, how they handle it defines part of their character. One group who fails will use their failure to better themselves and others around them. They see failure as an opportunity, as a learning experience, and a chance to grow through each setback. To this group, failure motivates them to push harder going forward. Then you have the group that struggles with their failures and in the process brings others close to them down. They do not see failure as a learning experience and usually, in their minds, it is not their fault. That leads them to look for excuses and comfort; we have all heard the phrase "misery loves company."

I am sure you see both of these traits in family members, friends or acquaintances. Where it gets difficult is when we ask ourselves what category we fall in. It is hard to be completely objective when we ask ourselves such challenging questions. When I have had these discussions, I have rarely heard someone say that they were unable to learn from failure and brought others down so that they would feel better. Who would admit to that? It is like asking someone you just met, are you a nice person or a mean person? No one thinks they are mean, they think others just do not fully understand them.

There was a Nike commercial years ago in which Michael Jordan was walking from his car into the arena to prepare for an upcoming game. As he is walking, we hear him listing all the shots he has missed in his career, from normal game shots to game winners. He is describing to us all of his failures. At the very end of the commercial, after listing his last failure as a basketball player he says, "And that is why I succeed."

Did you know that in competitive environments failure is more common than success? I love it when I say this and people look at me with a blank look on their faces like I just said something in another language. In baseball, a player that has a .300 batting average is considered good. That means out of ten at bats, they only succeed three times, failing the other seven times. In sports like tennis or golf you will lose more than you will win, that's just reality. In a sport like basketball, which I played, a team will usually miss more shots than it makes. If a player or team shoots fifty percent, then we consider that a game well played. To Michael Jordan, arguably the greatest player to ever play the game, it was a great game.

I come from a family of businessmen. When it comes to sales, they know that it is a numbers game. You might get ten rejections before you finally get a positive response. See what I am getting at here? We will fail a lot more often than we will succeed, so we have to know what category we fit into and learn how to use it to our advantage. It is the trait that separates those who do and those who wish.

When Failure Brings Us Down

Failure is a monster. It has the ability to grab hold of us and not let go. Failure is also contagious; we can get used to the feeling of failure. The mindset of those who let failure bring them down is simple: they learn how to adjust to failure instead of trying to learn and better themselves because of it.

Do you know someone who seems to have mood swings constantly? One day you see them and they are as happy as can be, then the next day you swear they have been replaced with some robot because their mood is totally different? People who have these mood swings wear emotions on their sleeve and, if they are trying to hide it, they often do not succeed. I come across these mood swings daily and have tried hard to understand where they come from and why. What I have learned is that failure has entered their lives on some level and what we witness is the reaction. What I also have learned is there are two types of feelings associated with a person that allows failure to bring them down. The first type is emotional failure, where individuals wear their emotions and it is obvious. Happy to sad, glad to mad, smile to a frown, outgoing conversations to short one word answers. The second type is scary. This is when individuals are used to failure and dealing with it, so their moods do not change, instead they slowly bring others down around them because that makes them feel a little better about their own struggles.

I deal with emotional failure ninety percent of the time when working with athletes. Their moods seem to align with their results. When they are winning or performing well they are happy fun people to be around. When they are losing or playing poorly, then I put the ten-foot rule into effect, meaning I give them ten feet of space, and if they want to initiate conversation they will call me over. This type of response to failure is common in our daily lives as well. When our day goes smoothly, the dinner table is a fun place to be. However, if we have a day we would like to forget sometimes it is better to eat in our bedrooms. I am not a psychologist but I do know that when we can control our emotions and use failure as fuel, rather than a distraction, our chance of success increases greatly. So how do we do that?

Usually when a person's emotions ride on results, they are having priority conflicts. It happens to me all the time. I find that I am more concerned with being successful in my everyday activities rather than those activities that lead to everlasting life. When I sit back and realize what I am doing, I get mad at my foolishness. If there is one thing I should know more than others, it is that competitive achievements, trophies and other accolades are temporary and only make us feel good for a short time. On the other hand, everlasting life is forever and will fill us with joy for eternity. With that in mind, do you think we should get so upset at every failure we experience, especially when it has nothing to do with our faith and relationship with Jesus Christ?

To get off the emotional roller coaster, we need to get back to the basics of what is most important in life. God does not care about the outcome of a competition; He cares how we conduct ourselves and how we compete. If we get down on ourselves He tell us this in Isaiah 41:10:

"So do not fear, for I am with you; do not be dismayed, for I am your God; I will strengthen you and help you; I will uphold you with my righteous right hand."

Doesn't that sound encouraging? That when we fail and think we are awful we can read that verse and understand that we are not alone; God is with us and He will strengthen us, which will help us improve and keep moving forward.

Be careful of what you are worshiping and where you are putting all of your emotions. A day will come where even the highest of competitive accomplishments will be lost and mean nothing.

The second type of response to failure I mentioned is when people use failure to bring others down. I do not deal with these personality types often, but when I do it is extremely difficult. You cannot see it coming, it is an invisible darkness that is going on around you and most of the time, when you finally realize it, the damage has already been done. Imagine someone who has an opinion about everything. They are happiest when things are done their way. They are always gossiping, talking about others, their faults, and the things they don't do instead of focusing on the positive things others may be doing. These individuals thrive on chaos, drama and others' misfortune. Why? Because when they cause drama, they are usually at the center of it and the attention comes back on to them. Proverbs 4:16 describes them this way:

> *"For they cannot rest until they do evil; they are robbed of sleep till they make someone stumble."*

Some people have the mentality that if they cannot do something, then neither should you. If they cannot be happy, then you shouldn't be happy either. If they have a bad marriage, then they will nitpick at yours until they find a vulnerable spot. Get the point?

Again, I don't have a degree in psychology, so I cannot tell you why some people are this way. But I can tell you that in competitive environments you will find people who will use their failure to bring others down around them. As the verse in Proverbs says, they cannot function unless they create chaos. When you find yourself with a person like this, it is up to you to have your priorities in the right place and know what to worry about and when to let go. I've found that these personality types are looking for you to react. They are trying to make you uncomfortable. When you react, and if they get under your skin then they have succeeded. If you know what is important, and have your priorities in the right place, then you cannot fail because such menial things will

not be worth your time, as they shouldn't be.
Using Failure to Succeed

I am working on this book during the greatest sporting event of the year (in my opinion), March Madness. If you do not know what March Madness is, then please ask a friend. I was watching a game where a number three seed was playing a fourteen seed, which usually means the game will not be very competitive. This game was different though; the team that was supposed to lose was actually playing quite well. As the game neared the end, the announcers informed all of us viewers that if the fourteen seed could hang on to win, it would be the first tournament victory in its school's history. All of sudden the game had my attention. I watched with interest and was delighted when the team did go on to get their first ever tournament victory. After the game, the head coach was interviewed and I was floored when he said that, at the beginning of the season, he had to dismiss his two best players from the team over a school infraction. I quickly got my notebook out and started to write down all of the competitive emotions his team must have experienced and the comparisons to this book.

When we face failure we face adversity. At that point we have a choice to make. We just discussed how we could let failure and adversity bring us down, now let's talk about how it can allow us to succeed.

The team that I watched get its first tournament victory faced adversity early in its season, so I am sure many thought just making it to the tournament would be an accomplishment in itself. I mean, come on now, if the school had been putting basketball teams on the floor for decades without

any tournament success then what would make anyone think this team, without its two best players, would be able to accomplish such a feat? I did not follow that team during the season, but I have a very good idea of their character. They never gave up, obviously did not compare themselves to others, but rather set their own standards, and they must have had a tremendous amount of belief in themselves and desire to not let any setback derail their dreams.

We could all learn from that example. Failure and adversity is imminent and sometimes out of our control. Our reaction, however, is not. When adversity arises we have a choice to make, and that is completely within our control.

The best choice you can make is the decision to learn and look ahead, not dwell and live in the past as told to us in Philippians 3:13

> *"Brothers and sisters, I do not consider myself yet to have taken hold of it. But one thing I do: forgetting what is behind and straining toward what is ahead..."*

In that verse, Paul was expressing to the Philippians that we all have things from our past that we are ashamed of, but that is not important. What is important is that we understand we are forgiven and we must move forward in our relationship with God.

Have you ever felt ashamed of something you have done in your past? Maybe a specific action you took or the way you treated someone? If you have repented, guess what? It's over. It is in the past and God has forgiven you for it. Don't you think it's time you forgive yourself?

I believe there are four things that separate those who use failure to succeed and those who let it bring them down. Those who use failure to move forward ask and understand these questions:

1) **Why did it happen?** You have to decipher if the failure was a result of something you did or something that was completely out of your control. Once you know that answer you can move forward to the next step.
2) **What can I learn from this failure?** When adversity strikes, there are lessons to be learned. If your actions contributed to the failure then it is important you know what specifically those actions were. Those who succeed do not make the same mistakes twice, they learn and move forward, and are smarter and have a greater knowledge of what to do and what not to do. If the failure was out of your control then you need to assess who was involved, why and how it affected you. Maybe it was something you did not specifically do but rather a situation you put yourself in. Either way it affected you and you need to know why and become wiser for the experience.
3) **How do I make sure it doesn't happen again?** The common sense approach would be, do not do that again, but it is rarely that easy. Whatever your tendencies are toward failure, the key to overcoming is education. If we do wrong then we need to educate ourselves on what is right. If golf is your sport and you always slice the ball then you have to educate yourself on how to fix your technique so you can hit the ball straight. If you come up short

when comparing yourself to others then you have to educate yourself on how to be humble and be thankful for what you do have, not what you do not have. No matter the fault, the key to overcoming is educating yourself on what the right thing to do is.

4) **How can I turn this failure into a success**? A lot of times failure humbles us, as it should. The main characteristic of those that turn failure into success is humility. By humility I mean that they do not feel like they are above anything. When top athletes fail they know they have to work harder, become wiser and believe in themselves like never before. They definitely do not sit around and make excuses, they internalize their mistakes and it motivates them to stay in the gym an hour longer than usual. Regardless of the situation they do not feel entitled, they feel humbled and blessed to have the opportunity to make up for their mistakes, to improve and become a better all-around individual.

You will fail at something within days of reading this chapter. Maybe it will be a small failure or maybe it will be big one. However big or small, I challenge you to ask yourself these four questions so that you can learn from it and turn it into a positive experience for your self-growth. Do not sit around in misery and look for some company to join you. We are drawn to those who build us up, not tear us down. When you face adversity you're not alone, so do not look at it as punishment. You are not special nor being singled out by God; we all face it. The worst thing you can ask yourself is "Why me?"

Why Not Me?

Nine years ago, on my birthday, I was at my grandparents' house along with all of my aunts and uncles. It was a time reserved for the adults in the family but my father had an engagement he could not miss so my mother stayed with him for support and I went up as our family representative, you could say. No matter if my parents were there or not I probably still would have buttinskied (a word I made up because I am always butting into things) myself into the situation. We were not there to celebrate my birthday; we were all there because my uncle was getting medical test results back that day. When he came back from the doctor's office, our biggest fears were realized: he had cancer and six months to a year to live. It was a sad day. I had an opportunity to spend about four quality hours alone with my grandfather that night. It was an intimate time for us. We talked, we both cried and I did my best to support him as he absorbed the realization that his son, my uncle, was going to die.

Fast forward about six months later. My uncle is hanging in there, going through treatments and staying positive. I am eating dinner one evening and I get a phone call from my grandfather. That was not unique, but what was odd was the fact that both my grandfather and grandmother were on line together, each on a separate phone in their house. We had the usual small talk, the "How are you doing, how is work going?" - and then the news came. He told me that he had cancer and it did not look great. I honestly do not remember anything more about that conversation; I just remember that I cried all night long.

I spent the next few months spending as much time as I could by my uncle's and grandfather's side. I wanted to help in any way I could and I always wanted to be around. During those times I had the opportunity to have one-on-one conversations with my grandfather, and one of those talks particularly stood out. I was probably complaining about the unfairness of the situation, wondering how both my grandfather and uncle could be dying of the same disease. In the middle of my complaining my grandfather stopped me and said, "Do not ever ask yourself **why me**, instead ask yourself **why not me**?" Excuse me? Come again? For the next hour he went on to explain the importance of attitude and how fortunate we are for the things that we do have in life, and not to focus on the things that we don't. It was during that conversation that we discussed Proverbs 15:33:

> *"Through fear of the Lord a man gains wisdom,*
> *and humility comes before honor."*

That verse has become and always will be my favorite, due to its meaning and the context in which I heard it. I want to share with you a little of the knowledge my grandfather shared with me that afternoon.

My grandpa was a front door type of guy. He told it like he saw it, and when he got going he let it all out. He took that moment to love me, lecture me, and humble me. That afternoon I had a negative mindset, rather than looking at all of the positive things taking place. He went on to explain to me that as a father he experienced every joy a father could have. He had six children who were all good people, had strong marriages, had a relationship with God and knew right from wrong. He talked about how our family had been blessed many times over and that our current sadness was a testament of how blessed we actually were. He wanted me to understand that up until that point, we as a family had not experienced loss or a tragic event. To him God was good, God was great, and he was thankful that God had looked over our family and given us the opportunity to live life as one for so long. It was important to him that I understood God owed us nothing, yet we owed Him everything. He told me that God would give us the strength to face every trial and to never ask "why me," but rather to ask "why not me." If I continued to ask "why me" then I would be foolish and arrogant. I would, in essence, be saying to God that I was above His wishes and desires. My grandfather would not allow me to have that mindset.

We have all been there. An event will rock our world and we will ask ourselves over and over, ***why me***? Please take a cue from the conversation that my grandfather and I had that afternoon. No matter how dire a situation may seem, remember that you are blessed, just maybe in ways that you do not realize. It is easy to look at what is wrong with our lives, but those who overcome and succeed are those that do not look for handouts or pity, instead they look at all of the opportunities they do have in life and feel fortunate for each and every one. God is good, God is great, He does not owe us anything. We owe Him everything.

Parents, Coaches, Mentors

What is your responsibility in all of this? It starts at the top and that means you! Every one of us deals with failure in some way, so it is imperative you know how to deal with it, because those we influence are watching our example. If you feel like you deal with failure in non-constructive ways then it is important that you first realize it, then secondly fix it. As a parent, coach or mentor, we cannot expect others we influence to handle failure with grace and class if we cannot set that example for them to witness. How we react to situations that happen to us is how we will be defined.

When it comes to teaching, we need to express the importance of staying in the present, not living in the past or the future. When we react it is usually to something that **has** happened, not something that will happen. What is important to understand is that reacting to something that **has** happened will not change the outcome. Changing the outcome of something that **has** already happened is impossible. So any negative emotion that we express is wasted energy.

I am constantly teaching this to athletes I train. I understand everyone is wired a little differently, so I tell my clients they have to be one of two ways. They either have to let things go and have an even temper, which some athletes have. Or if they are naturally emotional, they have to get just as excited about their successes as they do their failures. In working with athletes that play individual sports, such as tennis or golf, I see negative body language constantly. When they hit a bad shot or play a bad point they get on themselves and their frustration is evident. On the other hand, when they do something good there is no emotion, like "what's the big deal, I am supposed to hit good shots." This confuses me! I try to get one major point across: If you are going to get down on yourself for your mistakes, then you must build yourself back up through your successes. If an athlete fails to do this then he or she is only spending one type of energy, negative. If they are spending only negative energy, then where do you think their mindset is? You're right; they are focused solely on what they don't do compared to what positive things they are doing. That is the beginning of a downward spiral, which leads to a lack of confidence, the loss of happiness and a constant state of negativity.

All of this is not limited to athletics or competition. Youth today will experience failure in school, friendships, relationships, etc. It is vital that we are there for them in all areas of their life, helping them realize what is truly important. I try to instill a belief that no matter what, if you keep learning from your mistakes and forging ahead then you have already won half of the battle. You are already ahead of half of the people out there in this world. Proverbs 24:16 says:

> *"For though the righteous falls seven times, they rise again, but the wicked stumble when calamity strikes."*

Even back in biblical times, they knew about constant failure. No one is perfect, everyone sins and makes mistakes. But that is not the issue. God wants us to teach others the importance of learning from their past and how to forge ahead into their future wiser from their mistakes. If we trust in Him, He will strengthen and lift us up. Sometimes we have to look at ourselves and understand that it is okay to stumble. We also have to understand that if we learn from our failures, we will eventually find success. We must learn how to identify what success truly is and how to handle it once we attain some form of it.

Tasks

1) Write down the last time you remember failing and how it made you feel.
2) When you fail do you blame others or look at yourself internally?
3) Write a paragraph explaining how you can use failures in your life to your advantage.
4) Do you use a lot of wasted negative energy when you fail? If so, explain how that makes you feel afterward.
5) List five things you can do differently to build someone up, rather than bring them down, in times of failure.

Chapter 6

Success, What is it?

This is one of the most interesting questions that I ask athletes I work with. It is a simple enough question. But I can ask ten different athletes and I will get ten different responses. Now, you might think that if I was in a youth group setting at a church and I asked this question to ten different athletes in attendance, I might get a more uniform response. I wish that were the case, but ironically when I ask athletes who are confessed believers, they glance at me like it is some trick.

If someone had asked me that question when I was growing up, I would have given an answer that would have made my mentors cringe. Success to me meant winning basketball championships, playing at the college level and having all the attention that went along with it. If someone had asked me to point out a successful person, I would have nodded in the direction of the Michael Jordan poster on my wall. I had it all wrong back when I was growing up. I never really gave much thought to what success actually meant. When I felt like things were going well in my life, then I probably felt successful. On the other hand, when things were rocky I probably felt like I was far from being a success. As I started to mature, I found it ironic how people would mistake hollow imitators for success. I have had a few moments in my life where I have been congratulated or patted on the back for, in others' eyes, being successful when on the inside, my heart and soul felt anything but.

One summer, when I was in college, I was back in my hometown working out in the gym when a few kids that were there asked if they could watch. I said they could, so they sat on the side just watching and talking among themselves. After a few minutes I had the feeling they didn't just want to watch so I asked them if they would like to join me and shoot some baskets. They said yes, and for the next half hour or so they found contentment in rebounding and passing me the ball, which I loved because it allowed me to get up twice as many shots as I could have if I were alone. After a half hour or so I believe the kids felt a little more comfortable because their rebounds and passes were replaced with lightning-fast questions. Once I realized they were more interested in talking than rebounding, I called it a day and chatted with the kids as I packed up my bag. When I was leaving one of the kids asked me, "How can I be successful like you?" I will never forget that question because at that time in my life I was anything but successful. I was struggling in college and transferring to another, my grades were not the best and I had no idea what the future held for me and the little career I was trying to hold onto. I just looked at the kid and mustered a smile and said, "Do me a favor and do not try to be like me. Strive to be a lot better than I ever could be." I then walked away and thought to myself how backwards we really do think. That was a point in my life where I was not very diligent in my faith, so thoughts did not go there; rather they went to imagining how we can look at someone and think he/she are successful even though we have no idea what is going on in his or her life or where his or her heart truly lies. I didn't blame the kid for asking me, but I realized how fickle our view of success is.

Skip ahead a few years. I am not in college anymore, rather, working and sitting at a restaurant eating dinner alone. Here is what happened; I was sitting at a table, eating my food when a family came and sat behind me. I did not notice them or pay much attention as they walked by but their words I heard loud and clear. A little boy, maybe seven or eight, was asking his father all types of questions regarding the restaurant and making comments about how cool it was. The boy's sisters started to chime in as well and give their praise and they were as happy as three kids could be. That may not seem out of the ordinary but what struck me as odd was the fact that we were at a fast food restaurant, nothing fancy, and the kids were acting like they had never been there before, or if they had it was not something they were used to. As I continued to listen and pay more attention to their table I heard the father ask his son if he would pray before they ate their meals. The boy agreed and his prayer began. I wish I had a tape recorder or a better memory so I could recite to you his exact words. I had neither that night so I will summarize it the best I can. The boy thanked God for a great day, for his parents, grandparents and sisters, and then the shocker that got to me. He thanked God for his dad working hard so they could go out to eat as a family for his birthday since they never can afford to do so. The boy finished by saying "amen" and the whole family, in unison, followed with their own "amen." After the prayer, the mother said to the children that they should be thankful that God allowed their father to pick up some overtime hours so that they could enjoy the night out. I quickly turned around and looked at the faces of every family member sitting at that table. What I saw was a family that was happy and felt fortunate to be at a fast food restaurant, eating out, celebrating a birthday. My thoughts immediately went back to that day in the gym, years before, when some kid asked me how he could be successful. I am not sure why it got to me so much, but I had to leave the restaurant because I was getting emotional. I drove away thinking about all the things in my life I took for granted and how someone could look at me and think I was successful. It baffled me when I tried to comprehend how we view success. Nobody would look at that family sitting in the restaurant and consider them successful. They had on hand-me-down clothes and the father looked all greasy yet they had the most pure and successful spirit I had witnessed in a long time. How had I become so shallow? Where was my success meter?

Have you ever had one of those, "where is my success meter" moments like I had that evening? At that time, my walk with the Lord was shaky at best as I was just learning what the Bible and God were all about so I could make my decisions on how seriously I wanted to take it. I had just witnessed a family thanking God for allowing them to eat a $2 cheeseburger and because of it I was a wreck. I felt ashamed and every other emotion associated with guilt. I had to know more. I had to know why they had had so little yet were thankful for so much. I also had to know why I was so unthankful for what I had. I pondered those questions through the years and now that I have some experience under my belt, I have a better understanding of what success is and why others have such a hard time answering that question for themselves.

Athletes in today's society, whether they are believers of Christ or not, have the challenge of trying to understand what true success is. The hardest point to get across to young athletes is that one day their athletic career will be over and no one will really care how many trophies they have in their basement or how many scrapbooks they have full of newspaper articles praising their accomplishments. The day will come where they will be left with one thing and one thing only, their character as a person. Luke 6:24-26 touches on this topic:

"But woe to you who are rich, for you have already received your comfort. Woe to you who are well fed now, for you will go hungry. Woe to you who laugh now, for you will mourn and weep. Woe to you when everyone speaks well of you, for that is how their ancestors treated the false prophets."

It is difficult for younger athletes to grasp this notion because they have so much still ahead of them. When you are in the moment of something it is hard to realize that it will someday end. So, how do we deal with the tough task of helping athletes and individuals understand the true definition of success? First we have to identify what success actually means.

The Merriam-Webster dictionary online calls success a *"favorable or desired outcome".* It also calls success "**the attainment of wealth, favor or eminence (eminence means "position of power or superiority)".** The first part of the definition is where our success meter should be, but often times our meter is focused on the latter definition. Why is that?

The Wrong View of Success

As I mentioned in the beginning of this chapter, when I ask people what success means to them I get responses that range from having money in the bank to being married and having a nice house. If I ask young athletes this question I will get responses that talk about athletic accomplishments such as playing college sports or winning an upcoming game or tournament. Only once in a blue moon will I have an individual say that their relationship with God, how they treat others and how they carry themselves is what measures their success. When I get that response it is refreshing, but almost refreshing to a fault because it shows how unique that answer is.

We have touched on, in previous chapters, the challenges we face in teaching our youth the importance of knowing what their priorities are. This chapter is an extension of those same thoughts and practices. When we are teaching or looking at our own priorities we must also look at how we handle success once it comes. It is important that we do not let success change the person we are or the beliefs that we have. Sure, we all want to be successful in what we do, and again that is not wrong, but we need to understand where our time and efforts are being spent in the pursuit of success. In today's world it is easy to lose sight of what successes we should be trying to attain. Success is portrayed all around us, and usually in the wrong ways. We see advertisements that talk about living a better life through acquiring the latest smartphone, luxury car or bigger home. Those who make it to the top of their profession live lifestyles that we envy, although we have no clue what is inside their heart. When we go shopping at the mall, we see stores full of the latest clothes that we must have. Our friends take vacations so we feel that to measure up we must do the same. We constantly fall into the trap of not just wanting more, but needing more. Matthew 6:21 says:

> **"For where your treasure is, there your heart will be also."**

That verse makes it pretty clear that we need to make sure our treasure is one that will give us eternal life, not quick satisfaction. If we focus on things that have no real deep meaning or value, then that is where our hearts will be: meaningless. In today's culture newer is better, right? New may be better but it is also an illusion. We can go out and buy a new car, but it does not stay new for long. In athletics we can cherish our successes, but we need to realize that the feeling will only last a short time because we will play another game or match that we will lose. Eventually our career will be over. We have to have something deeper, more substantial to build our lives on. Do you know what is funny? I have seen and heard many conversations where people talk about the new car their friends bought or the vacation they just took. Usually when that happens I see the competitiveness come out and they will start talking about the things they wish they had or need in their life. Now, here is the funny and sad part. In witnessing conversations of that nature, I have never heard someone talk about their friends' or neighbors' faith and become envious to the point where they get competitive and have the urge to go out and get a faith like the ones their friends have. Have you? We have to fight the urge to want more because, in reality, the only thing we actually need is a relationship with God. He provides us with everything that we need. Everything else we have in life are wants.

Have you ever known someone who was a good person and acted in a way that you respected, only to see them and their behavior change once they reached some sort of success? I am sure we all have at some point in our lives. I know I have. It does not take much for an athlete to change his or her behavior once they achieve some sort of success. I have seen parents of athletes change once their child accomplishes certain feats. I have seen families do 180-degree turns in their lives once their father or mother reach some sort of success in their job. It is almost so common that it could be classified as a curse. That is why it is so unique when someone who does reach some form of success does not change who they are or what they believe in. Thanks to the culture we live in, once we have a little of something, we want more. This is never clearer than in athletic competitions, and young athletes are taking notice. With technology, kids have access to everything they could possibly want. They can see videos of how success has changed lives for athletes they look up to and they want some of that for themselves. Why are we like this? Two word answer, that question: Envy and selfishness.

What True Success Looks Like

Is it wrong to be competitive and want to win more championships or to make more money? No, absolutely not.

I hate to be a spoiler here, but that's not the whole answer. Remember when I asked you to rank your priorities and also rank what you spend time on during the course of a week? If we are becoming so obsessed with achieving objectives that have no long term effect on our spiritual growth, then the answer becomes "yes, it is wrong". I wholeheartedly believe that. God does not mind that we use our gifts and talents to be the best that we possibly can; after all, He gave us those gifts and talents! But He does mind when it takes away from being the person and follower He wishes us to be. 1 Timothy 6:17-19 sums this up pretty well:

> *"Command those who are rich in this present world not to be arrogant nor to put their hope in wealth, which is so*

> *uncertain, but to put their hope in God, who richly provides us with everything for our enjoyment. Command them to do good, to be rich in good deeds, and to be generous and willing to share. In this way they will lay up treasure for themselves as a firm foundation for the coming age, so that they may take hold of the life that is truly life."*

I read that verse and said, "Bravo, Paul". He was writing to Timothy offering encouragement. That verse lays it out really clearly. When Paul talks about the rich and putting hope in wealth he is speaking to all of us. He is instructing you and me not to be arrogant just because we may have nice material things in our life or superior athletic ability. Instead he is asking us to put our focus onto God, who will provide more certainty into our lives then we could ever find in any possession or talent that we may have. Then he instructs us to do good and be rich in good deeds, which means to use our talents and gifts that we have to benefit others, not just ourselves. Can you see the line being drawn in the sand?

At some point we need to stop - completely - and look at our lives and ask ourselves when enough is enough. In today's culture it doesn't matter if we make $30,000 a year or $100,000 a year, we will still have financial struggles. Why? Because our nature, as I have pointed out, is to want more when we have access to it. Imagine this scenario. A family makes $40,000 a year and lives off of that income. A few years pass and all of a sudden through hard work the family is now bringing home $70,000 a year. Do you think that they are still living as modestly as they were when they made $40,000 a year or do you think that their lifestyle may have changed a bit? Most of the time, in today's culture, our lifestyle changes as our circumstances do. God is begging us throughout the Bible to not fall into that trap. The possessions or trophies we acquire here on earth do not have any bearing on how successful we are. The true measure of success comes from our hearts and our one-on-one relationship with Jesus Christ. If you don't believe me then maybe Matthew 16:26 will help clear it up for us:

> *"What good will it be for someone to gain the whole world, yet forfeit their soul? Or what can anyone give in exchange for their soul?"*

No honor or award will allow us to enter through the gates of heaven, nor give us eternal life. While awards are good for our confidence, they mean nothing toward our salvation. The quicker we understand that, the quicker we will truly understand what true success is all about.

Parents, Coaches, Mentors

I am sure you probably have a pretty good idea of what I am going to say here. Yep, you guessed it; we need to take on society and do a better job in teaching young adults what true success is and how to attain it. It is a major fight and not one that we can take lightly. We have to stand up against technology, the media, Hollywood, and every other outlet that young people have access to.

Remember in the beginning of the chapter when I talked about being in youth groups and asking athletes in attendance, "What is success?" I normally get the same answers that I get from any other environment. Although sometimes I am surprised. When I am, it usually does come from a church setting. My point here is this: I do feel that children who are believers know what success truly is but they have become so used to seeing success portrayed in other ways that they get their wires crossed. When I ask them to tell me what success truly means, they get confused. It's like their brain knows what they want to say but their lips say something different. That is where the confused looks come from.

The weapons of battle that we need to fight this notion are purity and innocence. We have to do our very best to keep outside distractions in their rightful place, on the outside. We cannot shelter our children, but we can let them know from an early age what is acceptable and what is not. Psalm 119:9 says it this way,

> *"How can a young person stay on the path of purity? By living according to your word."*

It is imperative, if we are going to win this battle, that we teach those we influence the importance of innocence and purity. Those two words hold the key to understanding what true success is all about. In my mind, it takes one special trait to teach this to our youth: courage.

I recently had a conversation with my pastor, Pastor Ron, on the practice of inviting people to the altar during a church service to lay down specific sins. I observed that when a pastor invites people to the altar to lay something down the whole church should go up there, but yet only a few do. I told him that, in my mind, the only thing that separated those that go up when called and those who do not is courage. Some have the courage to walk up in front of others and profess that they are battling a certain issue in their life, and some do not. I proceeded to tell him that I felt it would be more beneficial to tell church members that after the service was over, pastors on staff would be hanging around in case anyone wanted to come and talk about any specific issues a person may be battling. Sounds easy enough, right? Well, I've realized something. I was wrong. Courage is a huge aspect of our faith, and it is not easy to come by. But when it comes to our faith, and if we are true followers of Christ, then we need to have courage to stand up and walk to the altar when called. If we go through life only expressing our faith in situations where we feel comfortable, then we are not true followers. The same goes for what I am asking you to do here when it comes to success.

When I am around young people and I ask them what success really means, I want them to have the courage to walk to the altar and say it is measured in one's personal relationship with God. I do not want someone to give me a popular answer then come up to me after everyone has left and then tell me what he or she truly believes success is. I want them to have the courage to be a true follower and give the answer that they know is right anytime and anywhere they are asked.

The same goes for you mentors. You will not be able to pass on the trait of courage unless you are willing to go against popular beliefs and have it yourself. If we do not have the courage to live it and pass it on, then we will lose the battle. Understand that if you have a child that is an athlete, at some point he or she is going to be out of your sight. Your children will be on team busses traveling to games or hanging out with friends after practice. In those moments, if we have not instilled them the trait of courage, then there is a good chance that their purity and innocence will be lost.

Young athletes and young adults need to have the ability to know what success truly means and the courage to stand up and pass it on to others rather than being influenced by the majority.

To follow God is not easy. To profess what you believe in uncomfortable environments is hard. To stand up for what you believe when heavily outnumbered is even harder. It cannot be done without the knowledge of knowing what true success is and the courage to live it. If we are to succeed, then know one thing: We won't always be the most popular people on the block and we must dare to be different from what society tells us we should be.

Tasks

1) Define what success means to you.
2) Have you ever had a "where is my success meter" moment? If so, please explain what that moment was and the circumstances surrounding it.
3) Explain some examples where you see the wrong portrayal of success.
4) Explain some examples where you see the right portrayal of success.
5) Have you ever had the courage to stand up for what you believe true success is? If so, explain the situation.
6) List three people that you would like to talk to about what the true meaning of success is.
7) Go talk to those individuals and write down how the conversations went.

Chapter 7

Dare to be Different

When I am working with young athletes, I am always hollering, "Dare to be different!" I would say that those four words are my motto when training athletes and the one thing I want them to understand most. If you have worked out with me before, then you know what I mean when I yell out that phrase. If you have not, then this is what I am trying to express. I want individuals to do today what they are not comfortable doing. I want today to be different compared to any other day. I want young athletes to do what others are not doing. I want them to run a few more sprints or stay 15 minutes longer than they are used to. I want them to give a little more today than they did yesterday and so on. If they have that mindset and do these things, then they will always be striving to do a little more - and that leads to progress.

In chapter four, we touched on the trap of maintaining. If I didn't push athletes to be different each day, then I would be creating an environment that accepts maintaining - and that is something I do not want. I do not want it for my athletes on the competitive field, nor do I want it for them in life. We can always be doing more and improving. When we improve as individuals, others around us often follow suit. They see us striving for more, doing more and as I discussed earlier, they do not want to be left behind, so they will join in. That leads us to the first phase of daring to be different: leading by example.

Dare #1: Leading by Example

As we talked about earlier, young athletes will always have an audience no matter what age they start competing. Because of that fact, they have a unique ability to learn the values of leading by example and having a positive impact through that process. In the previous chapters, we have discussed the traits of competitiveness and looked at examples of how we can use our platform to effectively influence others. We have to make sure that we have our priorities in the right place, which will allow us to be the type of competitor that others respect. I heard Lou Holtz say, "Titles come from the top, but respect comes from the bottom." What he means is that someone with authority to do so can name you team captain or the president of an organization. But that title doesn't automatically give you respect. Respect comes from those you are leading and serving. It has to be earned, and the best way to earn respect is to act in a manner others admire and want to emulate. In short, lead by example.

In my line of work, I see many different types of athletes. They range from just starting out and wanting to make some team to being at the top of the sport that they play and everything in between. You may think that I would prefer to work out with the top athletes because their skill set is so advanced. While I do find that to be enjoyable, it is not necessarily true. When I work out with an athlete for the first time, I have to spend the first thirty minutes mentally training them, explaining that they need to leave their ego at the door and not worry about how they perform but instead focus on learning and improving. Just like we do in the world today, everyone wants to make a great first impression and not appear weak or unable. What I try to explain is that I am not judging or grading on talent level, because talent is something that is out of our control. But I look at one's attitude, effort, and willingness to learn. Those are things that, no matter how little talent we have, are in our control and are the most important traits one can have - not just in athletics, but also in life. Most of the time the athlete thinks I am joking, but after thirty minutes or so they realize I am not, so they eventually stop trying to impress me and begin the process of learning and working hard.

Why is a willingness to learn, attitude and effort so important to me? Because ninety percent of the time individuals have it all wrong. We have fallen into the trap of thinking that talent and ability is what will get recognized and eventually rewarded. From experience, I can tell you, I have never been associated with a team where an individual with the most talent was named leader or team captain. I can tell you that the individual that had the best attitude, work ethic and desire to serve others was, one hundred percent of the time, named the leader and team captain. The lesson to be learned here is that those traits are a choice; they are not something we were born with. ***Leading by example takes no talent at all***; it just comes down to a choice that we have to make. If you want to make a positive impact on others or be someone that others admire, then all it comes down to is a choice, made by you, to lead through your actions - not your talents or knowledge.

This rings true when it comes to our faith as well. In college I saw many examples of people who felt their knowledge earned them the right to lead or be a mentor. I would have conversations where people would try to impress me with their ability to memorize Bible verses or by challenging me to the game of who can find a book of the Bible the quickest, almost like we were gunslingers of old. I would tell those people that one's knowledge of Bible verses or ability to open a Bible to a specific book quickly, while impressive, had no bearing on what I thought of them as a person or spiritual leader. That was determined by the way they carried themselves, the impact they had on others and the ability to lead though their example. Do you feel your faith is based on, at times, what you know instead of what you do and the example you set? Do you find yourself feeling like you do not have to prove anything to anyone because you know that when no one was watching you put in the hours and trained hard to be the best person you could be? While that is good, it is not what God wants for us. He urges us to go out and take our knowledge and use it to impact others by our actions and examples as is stated in James 2:14-17:

> *"What good is it, my brothers and sisters, if someone claims to have faith but has no good deeds? Can such faith save them? Suppose a brother or a sister is without clothes and daily food. If one of you says to them, "Go in peace; keep warm and well fed," but does nothing about their physical needs, what good is it? In the same way, faith by itself, if not accompanied by action, is dead."*

Or, if you would like a shorter version that you can memorize easier, how about Hebrews 13:16:

> *"And do not forget to do good and to share with others, for with such sacrifices God is pleased."*

And lastly, one of my favorites… Philippians 2:4:

> *"Not looking to your own interests but each of you to the interests of others."*

Are you impressed by my Bible verse, gun-slinging abilities yet? Don't be, I had time to research. In these verses, a message is made clear. What we have does not impress God; how we use it to benefit others does. And the best part of all is this: to please God and lead by example does not take any talent or wealth, it comes down to a choice to learn, to share and then do. If I had the chance to spend the next year speaking to a different group of competitors each day, I would try to drive home this important point. An individual's attitude and mindset will be the determining factor for so many things in his/her life. I want him/her to understand that their example will have a far greater reach and impact on others than their talent ever will.

So my first dare to all of you competitors, athletes and parents is this: I dare you to be different and to lead by example. I dare you to make an impression, not with your words but rather through your actions. Create an environment where one sees the ability to do good through the choices he/she makes, not the talents they have. (remember when I discussed youth excelling in consistent environments? It's all coming together, like a circle, it's all related to one another.) As Titus 2:6-8 says,

"Similarly, encourage the young men to be self-controlled. In everything set them an example by doing what is good. In your teaching show integrity, seriousness and soundness of speech that cannot be condemned, so that those who oppose you may be ashamed because they have nothing bad to say about us."

Do you feel it is impossible to live to such a standard? Here is some food for thought. What negative things do they say about Tim Tebow? That he doesn't throw a football properly? Maybe people say that his faith distracts others on his team? Whatever the case may be, in the scheme of life are those really negative comments?

Dare #2: Give a Little More

Ask yourself what separates you from the rest; how are you different? I am sure you can list a few things that you feel separates you from others, but there is one choice you can make right now that will separate you from 90% of people in this world. Do you know what that is? It is the trait of learning how to give a little more than you are used to giving.

When I am training an athlete of any age, I always try to get them to give just a little more than they think they can give. As individuals we push to a limit that we feel is our max - our maximum effort, where we think it would hurt to give any more. We don't like pain and when we think doing something is going to be painful, our brain sends us a message to stop. This holds true when I am working with an athlete. I will put them on a treadmill and set the speed at a comfortable pace. Five minutes into their run I will raise the pace to a point that is uncomfortable to them and say, "Tell me when you cannot go any further." Usually within 30-60 seconds they are telling me they cannot go any further. Then I say, "Give me 15 more seconds, you can do it." It's amazing, but they are always able to give me 15 more seconds. When I lower the speed back down to a walking pace, I emphasize that they just gave me 15 seconds more than they thought they could give. I will usually repeat the exercise two or three times and ask them to give me 20 seconds more, then 25 seconds more and so on. Two things happen when we are finished with this exercise. One, they are proud of their accomplishment and feel good about themselves. Secondly, my point is proven without me having to say a word. They realize that they can give a little more and it sets the tone for the rest of the day.

You may be familiar with the movie created by a church in Georgia, "Facing The Giants". If not, I highly recommend that you rent or buy it. There is a scene in the movie where the football team is on the field practicing. The head coach is talking to the players about the upcoming game when one of the players makes a comment about how much better their opponent is. The coach asks the player if he thinks they have already lost. The player gives a halfhearted response. The coach then asks the player to come forward and do the death crawl with a teammate on his back (that is when a player uses just his hands and feet and crawls by lifting his knees just off the ground so they are not touching). The coach asks the player to give his very best, so the player agrees to do so. When the player is ready and in position the coach asks how far he thinks he can go. The player says 30 yards. The coach replies by saying he thinks he can go 50.

The coach throws in one last challenge by blindfolding the player so he cannot see how far he has gone. The player begins, goes 30 yards, then 50 yards, then 70 yards and keeps going as his coach is urging him to give his very best. When the player cannot go any further the coach urges him some more, to not quit, that he wants his very best and that he can do it. The player continues on till he cannot give any more. He falls down, takes his blindfold off only to see that he was in the end zone. He went the full length of the football field - 100 yards.

I love that scene, and I have started to incorporate the blindfold technique into some of my training. Sometimes when athletes I train are on the treadmill, I will put a towel over the screen so they cannot see their time, how fast they are going or how far they have run. I will set a goal, encourage them and when it's all over I remove the towel. When they glance down to the screen, they are amazed at what they accomplished and how they surpassed their goal.

So, how can we push ourselves to give a little more when we do not have the luxury of someone placing a towel over our eyes and motivating us? It starts with baby steps. Each day we have to make the choice to give a little bit more than we did yesterday. It is like a diet. Why do they fail? Most of the time a person makes a decision that they want to diet and lose weight. So one day they wake up and say this is going to be the day and they begin the process of eating healthier and cutting out all of the foods that have brought them to this point in their life. Where diets fail is when expectations are too high and people expect years of a certain lifestyle to change overnight. It is not realistic. Instead of slowly taking baby steps and cutting harmful foods out one by one, they go for the whole gusto. Eventually that leads to cravings and hunger pangs, which then leads to a pig-out session. When it comes to our lives, we need to learn from diets that fail. If we can take one step at a time and learn to give and do a little more today than we did yesterday, then a point will come where we will look back, 30, 60, 90 days down the road, and see how much of an impact the incremental changes we made have had on our lives.

Another aspect of giving a little more includes helping and giving unto others. It is not our place to judge, but rather to help others succeed. If we all took the initiative to help create positive change through our actions then we would immediately be doing more than we are accustomed to. Imagine if everyone in your city or town took one day to give a little more of their time, attention, money, kindness and compassion. Do you think it would pay huge dividends on the morale of the community? I think it would be amazing. It is also important to note that if you are on a team then you should put more stock into your team's success than your own. We get back what we give. How can we feel complete if our only motivation comes from our own personal success? 2 Corinthians 9:6 touches on the matter when it states,

> *"Remember this; Whoever sows sparingly will also reap sparingly, and whoever sows generously will also reap generously."*

Again, giving a little more than you're used to is a choice, it takes no talent at all. The choice is yours. Are you going to maintain and do what you are used to doing, or are you willing to give a little more and do things a little differently?

Dare #3: Do Things Differently

So here we are. You have made a choice that you dare to be different. You want to be a leader by example and you want to give a little more. The tool that ties all of those decisions together is the last step: doing things differently. It comes down to common sense, right? If you continue doing things as you have done them before, then you would get the same result. If you are making a decision to be more of a leader by example, use your platform more effectively, care without really caring or any other challenge that this book has discussed, then you are choosing to do things differently.

I know this sounds too simple, but the reality is: we dislike change. I could use another word, surprises. We like things the way they are, we fall into a routine and if things are going okay, why would we think about changing or doing things differently? Most of us fall into one of two categories: either we don't think about doing things differently because things are okay as is, or we think about doing some things differently but never really get around to making actual change. If that is the case, then how do we do things differently?

To make change requires action. Remember the principle we have heard thousands of times, "every action causes a reaction". Well that logic fits this bill perfectly. If we are going to do something different, then we have to make the choice to do so. That is the first step in the action process. The second step is the actual new or different thing we do, and then the reaction follows. You with me so far? Good.

Although doing things differently can sometimes be a difficult process, the rewards can be very fulfilling. If we choose to make a change, and it comes from a good heart, then we will find ourselves making a change to be a better person, not just for ourselves but for those around us. That is an unselfish gesture on our part. If we decide to make change for selfish reasons, then it will be shown through our examples. What do I mean? If an athlete comes to me and we have a discussion about change, I will not focus on the things they wish to change but rather on the reasons why. If they tell me that they wish to be better so they can set a great example and use their platform and influence others in a positive way, then I feel they are making an unselfish decision and one I fully support. On the other hand, if an athlete tells me he or she wishes to change because he or she wants to be better and the focus is solely on him or her, with no thought on any bigger picture, a red flag pops up for me. It is not wrong of them to want change so they can become better, but it is wrong if it is only about them, and here's why. When a person is making change, solely for their benefit, then they are too result-oriented. Rather than focusing on the process of change, they look for immediate results. When athletes get in this mindset, they are usually looking for fixes. I compare a fix to a Band-Aid. A Band-Aid is a temporary device that helps something heal. Instead of making the choice to do things differently and focus on the process of improvement, they go through life always looking for a Band-Aid. When a problem arises they just stick on a Band-Aid in hopes that it will heal soon. A by-product of this mindset is an individual ruled by their emotions. He or she lives only for the here and now. When things are going well then so is their mood. When things go south, so does their demeanor.

Do you see any resemblance to our faith? Where we fall into the mindset of focusing on the here and now rather than the long-term process? We go through stretches where our faith meter points to full because we do the right things, take an unselfish approach to life and are humbled by what we have and feel blessed. We dive into God's Word and use our platform to influence others, the right way. Then we have those times where our faith meter points to empty. During those stretches, we are an emotional roller coaster. When things don't go our way, we react accordingly to the situations we find ourselves in. We believe in God but our actions tell a different story from where we want our heart to be. We succumb to the temptations around us, and the changing patterns of society.

In order to fix that cycle, we need to be different. We have to give a little more and do things differently today than we did yesterday, and so on. If everyone chooses to accept things as is and never challenges themselves to do more, then we lose control and leave things to chance. When it comes to life, our faith and any athletic accomplishment we are trying to achieve, we need to take control and create our own course, not follow one that has been traveled on many times before us as told in Romans 12:2:

> *"Do not conform to the pattern of this world, but be transformed by the renewing of your mind. Then you will be able to test and approve what God's will is - his good, pleasing and perfect will."*

Parents, Coaches, Mentors

Remember the Tim Tebow story I told you? The one where he wore a Bible verse under his eyes during the national championship game his junior year and the verse he wore was Googled 94 million times. There is a little more to that story. During the football season that year the verse that Tim wore for most of the season was Philippians 4:13:

> *"I can do all this through him who gives me strength"*

It wasn't until the days leading up to the national championship game that Tim felt led in his heart to change the verse. Now that may not sound like a big deal to you, but remember, athletes and fans are superstitious. They don't like things changed up, especially if those things are working. Tim wasn't trying to fix anything; he was just trying to follow his heart. In the video I watched of Tim's speech, he talked about how his parents were very supportive about the change and how his coach trusted Tim to do what he felt was right even though he was a little more apprehensive. Who can blame him, right? If it isn't broke, then why fix it? As we now know, Tim did change that verse for that game and it did have an unbelievable impact. What did Tim do so special? He used his platform to send a positive message and he wasn't afraid to do something different that night.

Sometimes we as parents, coaches or mentors want to keep things "as is." We do not like to change and if we do accept some form of change, we usually have to be sold on it. That is not a terrible thing; however, I want to remind you of something we have already discussed: ***If you are not growing, then you are dying.*** It is essential that we feed ourselves with knowledge and continue to grow. One cannot grow without being open to change. I am not advocating that you go out and start changing everything in your life, but I am challenging you to look at your life and ask yourself why you do what you do, and how that impacts others around you. I can assure you, if we take a deep and honest look at our lives we will find something that could use improvement.

I think being different or looking to do things a bit differently is a good thing. If we urge our youth to be different, stand up for what is right and what they believe in, then we should be right there with them blazing a trail by example. I fall short of this often and it is something that I have to work on daily. In my life I find it hard to always eat the right things, work out as diligently as I should and so on. Well, that creates confusion in the youth I work with. There have been times where I am educating them on how to eat properly in the afternoon only to run into them in the evening at some restaurant while I am stuffing my face with pizza or a plate of fried foods. What kind of message do you feel that sends? If I had a quarter for every time I heard an athlete say to me, "Do as I say, not as I do, huh?", I would be a very wealthy man.

I am no different than anyone reading this book. I fail over and over and have to make a choice each day to lead by example and practice what I preach. I have a feeling we can all relate. I am not saying we cannot enjoy ourselves, I am just saying that if we want our youth to be different by doing the right things and leading by example then we have to make sure, we, too, are instilling the same principles within ourselves. It is important that we create a safe environment for those around us. An environment that lets people grow, lets them be open to trying new things, and lets them be different. What if Tim's parents had told him changing that Bible verse was a terrible idea? What if others around Tim begged him not to change that verse for the national championship game? Would the result have turned out differently? I do not think that would have been the case; however, I do believe Tim would have been conflicted and would have been questioning himself on what to do. It is not our place to make those around us question themselves when it involves positive change. It is our responsibility to encourage them to do what they feel is right, and support them in their growth, as Tim's parents, coaches and teammates did that evening.

I dare all of you parents and mentors out there to do something a little different. Maybe it's communicating a little better or more often with those within your platform. Maybe it is holding others around us a little more accountable. Whatever the case, I dare you to do things a little differently than you are used to. Without change, there is no growth.

Tasks:

1) Do you feel that you are different? If so, explain how.
2) Write down three things you feel you could do differently in your life that would make a positive impact.
3) Set a goal to incorporate three things that you are going to do differently in your life that you feel will be a positive influence for yourself and others around you.
4) Dare someone close to you to be different and make a change that you feel could benefit them.
5) Keep a journal or notebook and track, for one month, how your change has had an impact on not only you, but those around you as well.

Chapter 8

Passion

We all get emotional. Some of us cry at sad movies. When someone close to us is hurting, we may shed a tear or two. I am an emotional person, and there is one thing that gets me going every time: when I see people's dreams coming true. If I am watching one of those talent reality shows, you can bet at some point I am going to get choked up. I just love a story where a person never gives up hope, follows their dreams and does whatever they can to make them come true.

Imagine this for a moment. A contestant comes walking onto a stage and introduces him or herself. The judges ask what his or her goals are and, depending on the situation, sometimes the judges or crowd will sigh as if to say, "Good luck, we have heard this before." Then the contestant is given the green light to begin as everyone sits back expecting another outlandish dream to die. However, once in a while, the contestant will begin to perform and everyone is in awe. Their voice or dance steps captivate everyone and the silence that was once reserved for pity is now a sign of respect. Then, once the contestant is done, the crowd erupts, the judges are in shock and the contestant has a look that could light up the darkest of rooms. In some cases, they shed a tear right along with me.

Why does that get to me so much? Because it is so refreshing to see a dream become a reality. In my work, I too often see the opposite. I see potential go by the wayside because the athlete just couldn't find the desire or passion within to make their talents shine through. Sadly, it's very unusual to see individuals reach their full potential. It shouldn't be, but it is. I think that attests to the normal mindset we have always come to accept; that falling short of your potential is sometimes okay.

How do we turn that tide and try to help all those around us? How do we help those we care about so deeply reach their full potential and help make their dreams come true? We create passion, that's how.

First, let's look at the definition of passion, because I think we confuse passion at times. In the Merriam-Webster dictionary, the word ***passion*** has several different meanings, depending on the context in which it is used. The context we are looking for gives this definition: "a strong liking or desire for or devotion to some activity, object or concept." There also is a definition that describes passion as, "an object of desire or deep interest." Armed with that knowledge, we can now dive into how passion is a vital part of our successes as a person, athlete and competitor.

Passion is where it all starts. This topic could have been the first chapter in the book but I chose to put it off so we could examine our competitive nature and how to use it effectively. Without passion there is no desire to become better, make changes, be different or use any platform. I am guessing that if you are reading this book, then you have a passion to learn about the topics discussed, have a desire to change and that excites me. So if passion is where it starts, then when does it start in us? When we are young, our parents make decisions for us. When we are young individuals who compete, there is a good chance it is because our parents put us in that activity, not because we chose it. So at that time our parents had a passion for whatever activity they put us in, or our parents had a passion for us to be active so they put us in anything and everything to see what we enjoyed or excelled at most. In that process there came a point where we, as competitors, started to develop a passion for a particular activity. We would find our efforts and time becoming more focused on that activity, as other activities we were less passionate about fell by the wayside. All of that leads us to the present. What are you passionate about and why?

If you have a passion for something, it stems from one of a few things. Remember the questions I asked in chapter one and four: Why do you do what you do? Who do you do it for? Well those questions apply here as well. Some people have a passion for something because it's what they love to do; their passion comes right out of the dictionary. Some have passion for something because their friends or family have a passion for it so they follow along. Then, you have the people that at some point lost their passion but continue to plug along, go through the motions because they don't know what else to do. If you are in the first example, then you don't need much motivation. If you are one of the last two examples, then I challenge you to re-evaluate what you're doing.

If we have the opportunity to compete, then we have been blessed. There are many people in the world today that would love nothing more than to be a part of something bigger than themselves but will never have the chance due to circumstances. Do not take your abilities or fortune for granted. Do all things with passion, because anything less would be selling yourself short and one day you will feel regret. We talked about how the "what if" question paralyzes us mentally. If you are a young competitor reading this, then please understand one thing. One day it will be all over. One day you will find yourself sitting somewhere thinking back to the days when you had your parents and friends supporting your competitive efforts. You will realize that those days are long gone and in those moments you will start playing the "what if" game. You will think about things you should have done or could have done when you had the opportunity. However, if we dare to be different then when that day arrives you will look back with no regrets and be proud of your accomplishments, not be measured by the number of trophies you collected but by the number of friendships you made and lives you influenced through your example. If you are an adult or parent reading this, there is a good chance you have spent a night or two reliving your glory days; who hasn't, right? For us it is too late to go back to high school or college athletic competition, but we can positively feed the passion in those whom we care about. I might be dating myself here, but when I was in high school all of our games were taped on VHS camcorders. My mother kept every tape from my senior season, and a few years ago she had the memorable games converted to DVDs. She gave them to me as a present, and I was thrilled to have them. It is funny how I look at those tapes now compared to when I watched them years ago, right after graduating. I used to watch them and break them down over and over. I would study them and see things I did wrong or things I could have done better and probably actually thought that I might be able to go back and fix my mistakes (I didn't really think that but I did analyze my mistakes). Today I will pull them out, once a year or so, and watch them because it was a happy time in my life and when I feel I need to fill my passion tank, that is my fuel. I watch them so I can remember the time in my life when I had love and passion for what I was doing and how that affected my attitude. The truth is, we will go through times in our life where our passion meter is running low and it is important that we have something, or someone, that we can go to and get our passion tank refilled. Ask yourself what fills your passion tank. It is important to know so that when you need some refueling you know exactly where to go to fill it up. I can't tell you what that may be; only you know, but if you need a place to start, get out your Bible. I did not always practice what I suggest. I am a work in progress and trying to do the right thing each day. But maybe you can get a head start and learn from my mistakes.

My passion came from the love of what I was doing. When I was growing up, I played basketball with my uncles, shot hoops in the driveway with my father and I even played a few games of horse with my mother. I had great mentors, and I'm sure that added to my passion. When adults around me took interest in what I was doing, that fueled my drive even more. When I was in high school I heard a guy speak at a camp I attended and he told a motivating story. I have heard the story told a few times and in a few different ways through the years but the basics of the story remain the same. Recently I was sent a video entitled, "How Bad Do You Want It?" I believe it was done by the Hip Hop Preacher, and it told a similar message to that of what I heard years ago and was very inspiring, just like the version I heard at camp when I was younger. It went something like this.

A young man wanted to be successful; he wanted to be

successful like a certain man in town was. So one day the young man approached the guru and said that he wanted to be successful just like he was. The old man said, "If you want to be successful like me, then I will meet you tomorrow morning at the beach." The young man agreed and the following morning showed up at the beach. The old man said to him, "How bad do you want to be successful?" The young man said very badly, so the older man said, "OK, walk out into the water." The young man found it strange but walked out into the water till it was waist deep. The older man followed and said, "Walk out a little further." The young man did as he was told until the water was up to his chin. The young man turned around and said, "I want to learn how to be successful; I don't want to learn how to swim." At that time the older man took his hand, wrapped it around the young man and dunked him under the water. The young man got a little nervous, and as the older man held him under, the younger man started fighting, trying to get back up above the water. After a little more time had passed, the older man pulled him up above the water only to see the younger man gasping for air and yelling at how crazy the old man was for doing that to him. The old man said to him, "You want to be successful right? Well, when you get to the point where you want to be successful at whatever it is you do as badly as you want to breathe, then you will be successful. When you get to a point where you don't care about what your friends are doing, care about what is on the television or care what others think about you because all you care about is taking a breath then you will be successful."

There are times in our life where we find ourselves in a position where we do not care about anything around us other than finding a way to catch our breath and get some air. Being fortunate enough to see top athletes work out and perform, I have seen examples where the only thing they care about is being successful at what they do, on and off the playing field. They want to be the very best that they can be. In working with younger athletes, I cannot say that is the case most of the time. I see them run over to their phones, texting and checking their messages during the first break they get. I see them leaving early instead of staying late. I see them looking at the clock wondering how much longer they have in practice instead of wondering what extra reps they could get in after. Most athletes today kind of want it; they don't know what it takes to really want it. It always amazes me when I see athletes that have made it to the highest level, get paid millions of dollars working as hard as they can, only to see young athletes who want to make it to where their idols are, but only work half as hard. Shouldn't it be the other way around? It seems that once an athlete has made it to the top of their profession, they may take a little time off, get comfortable and slack off a bit. You'd think the younger athlete who wants to make it would be doing everything in his or her power to make sure they gave themselves every opportunity to make their dreams come true. Do you know what separates the two? In my experience, it is passion. Once we have passion then we can achieve success. Without passion there is no motivation to succeed.

Passion cannot be taught. It is something inside of us that motivates and drives us to push forward and get the most out of everything that we do. In life, in order to accomplish anything, we must be willing to sacrifice. If you're working toward something and investing time into your efforts, then get a reward from it. Do not do something halfheartedly and get no reward from the work you have already put in. Don't let distractions such as texting, your Facebook page, or what your friends think stop you from getting your rewards. It is your life, and you have made the necessary sacrifices, so go and make sure you get something out of it. That is one of the components that separate those who achieve and those who do not. Those who achieve push on, overcome obstacles and sacrifice to make sure that they get a reward for their hard work. Those that do not make it succumb to outside influences and give up. They are not willing to sacrifice certain things in their life, and when adversity or distractions arise, they stall and slowly come to a complete stop.

The same holds true when it comes to our faith. Many of us are not willing to sacrifice certain behaviors in our life to truly follow God and be the example that He wishes us to be. God wants us to do everything to the best of our ability as a way to honor Him as told in 1 Corinthians 10:31 and Colossians 3:17:

"So whether you eat or drink or whatever you do, do it all for the glory of God."

"And whatever you do, whether in word or deed, do it all in the name of the Lord Jesus, giving thanks to God the Father through him."

It is important to understand that although we may compete, some of us may not be doing it to play at the highest levels. Maybe we just like to compete, stay active and want to participate as long and as far as our abilities will take us. I want you to know, that is perfectly fine. In fact, it is admirable as long as you are giving your best effort in the process. My only suggestion is that you sit down with your parents, mentors or coaches and explain to them what you have a passion for and why you compete. If you have one goal and those around you have different goals for you, then you will find yourself miserable. Remember this equation:

Clear communication + Realistic expectations = Happiness.

Parents, Coaches, Mentors

I am going to get right to the point. Passion and believing in yourself (next chapter) are critical components to an individual's growth. We as parents, coaches and mentors play an important role in how those traits are developed in those around us. In most cases, those traits make the difference between someone fulfilling their potential and achieving their goals or falling short and playing the "what if" game down the road. If someone we mentor can have the passion and motivation to accomplish their goal, as well as the belief that they can succeed, then anything is truly possible. So how do we instill those traits and develop them in the right ways?

That is a very touchy question and one I've spent many, many, and I mean many hours talking about with parents and coaches. There is a very fine line between being pushy and giving a little push forward to help motivate a young person when they seem to be stuck. What I see all too often is a parent or mentor who has his or her hands on the steering wheel a little too tight. They are driving the vehicle and they just can't let go or loosen up. When something goes awry or they see faults and errors, they start scrambling for a solution. They are the opposite of caring without really caring; they care too much and that suffocates the young person at times. Now I want to be careful here because I do not want to sound preachy, so let me explain.
I think it is our responsibility to first and foremost make sure

that individuals around us have their priorities in the right place. Sometimes we lose sight of that and we become blinded to what we are actually doing or how we are behaving. When that happens we need a wake-up call. I have had many wake-up calls in my life, one pretty recent.

I was working out with one of my better athletes a while back and she was distracted - happy, but distracted. She was losing focus easily and I started to ride her a little bit, get after her and push her harder and harder, trying to get her to focus. Finally I stopped the workout and asked her what was going on – why she seemed happy but was not focusing. She told me she was excited because she had found out that she was going to be inducted into the National Honor Society at her school. I felt like someone had just punched me in the gut. There I was pushing, motivating and getting on her when she could care less because she just had this amazing accomplishment happen in her life. Embarrassed, I told her that I was very proud of her and that her accomplishments off the tennis court mean far more to me than any accomplishment she would ever have on it. We stopped the workout and just talked and celebrated for a little while.

I needed a wake-up call that day, and I got one. It is important that we keep asking ourselves, "Whose passion is it?" Our passion or the individual's we are trying to help and influence? There are exceptions to any rule, but in most cases if a parent or mentor pushes a child to succeed and the passion comes from them more than the person competing, then the outcome will eventually be failure. We can want it for them for only so long, because there will come a point where they start having a little more freedom and start making choices for themselves. And when that happens, what choices do you think they will make?

When a young person I train wins a game, tournament, or has success, I always try to search out the parents and congratulate them on their child's achievement. Sometimes they say thank you and are humbled by it, which is refreshing. Other times I get responses that make me cringe. The other day I congratulated a parent on her child's tournament victory and she didn't say thank you or flash a smile filled with pride. Instead she just looked at me and said, "Well, there is room for improvement; she can do better." I just sat back and smiled and said that she will get there, not to worry, while inside I was fuming. I get goose bumps, not in a good way, when we find ourselves at a point where winning is not good enough, because it isn't perfection. It is in those moments when the fine line is crossed. At that point, passion turns into obsession. Passion and obsession are two totally different things but tied together way too often. I have heard obsession defined as out of control passion. I agree!

I do not mean to sound like a broken record here but there are things we should be obsessed about in our lives. Our faith and how we treat others would be at the top of the list. We should not be obsessed on wins or losses but maybe rather on how we acted and the example we set. I have seen many great competitors win over and over but their attitudes and actions are a far cry from honorable. They don't see anything wrong with how they act because most of the time they are surrounded by enablers that let them get away with the obnoxious behavior. Most of those individuals have a rude awakening coming. There will be a point when they are not the best anymore and their talents are just average compared to those around them. When that happens they will have nothing positive to fall back on. They will not be a positive influence on others; they will not help

others succeed because their whole life has been about them. It's sad to see but their stories usually do not have a happy ending.

I just spoke about the equation,

Clear Communication + Realistic Goals = Happiness

This equation is for individuals and their parents and or mentors. It is very important that you and the young person that you influence are on the exact same page. Being on different pages causes confusion and frustration. It is not enough to assume you know what their goals and passions are. You need to know exactly what their goals and passions are. When I see the parent that is holding on to the steering wheel a little too tight, then I know for a fact that their goals and expectations are different from their child's. To get away from that behavior, set monthly or bi-monthly outings with your child or those you have an influence on. Go out to dinner or just sit down and talk. Review their expectations, what they are thinking, obstacles they are facing and communicate your thoughts. I promise everyone will be better off for it and you will find yourself in a healthier and happier environment.

We cannot make someone have passion; we can only help fuel their passion. Our responsibility is to be aware of what is important to those around us, make sure their priorities are in the right place and encourage them to be the best that they can possibly be. If we have tunnel vision for what we are passionate about then we will miss out on all of the great accomplishments that those around us have going on in their lives. We will lose sight of the fact that someone dear to us just made the National Honor Society because all we will care about is if they were focused on what matters to us. I am guilty of it, are you?

Task:

1) What are you passionate about? Do those close to you know what you are passionate about?
2) What do you do to fuel your passion when you feel like you are worn down?
3) Do you communicate your passion with a parent or mentor?
4) Do you feel you have passion or an obsession?
5) If you are a parent, do you talk to your children about what they are passionate about? If so, how do you nurture their passion and help it grow?

Chapter 9

Believe in Yourself… The Three S's

Growing up, my parents would always tell me I walked the fine line between being cocky and confident. I used to always say to them that if I didn't believe in my abilities, who else would? Looking back, I know I said that as a quick rebuttal because, in our household, debating is a trait we were all born with. The truth is I was cocky. I once had a college coach tell me that my mouth wrote checks that my body couldn't cash. "Ouch, easy on the Top Gun one liners, dude!" is what I wanted to say. But instead I was distraught, even furious. The truth was I believed in myself, but for all the wrong reasons. I believed in materialistic things, things that do not matter. I cared more about playing a college sport and all that came with it than I cared about being a good person, treating people with respect and using my platform to influence others in a positive way. If I could go back in time, there are so many things I would do differently. Don't we all wish we had three do-overs?

I want you to learn from my mistakes. I want you to understand that along with passion, the other critical aspect to growth is the ability to believe in yourself and being confident in what you believe in! I have talked about the circle, that everything in this book is related and the ability to believe in yourself starts with this book's golden rule; making sure your priorities are in the right place in order to use your talents, passion and platform in a positive way. When I am dealing with athletes and I see their priorities are in the right place, then I challenge them to live out the three S's:

Stand Up
Step Out
Shine

Before I explain what the three S's mean, we have to look at what it is we believe in.

What do you believe in?

I have a friend that drives me nuts. There is nothing wrong with him other than the fact that he is always in the middle of every debate that circles around him. He never takes a stance or has an opinion. When we were in college, he would just sit back and listen to one of the many nightly debates taking place and agree with both sides. One evening a group of us got together and decided that we were, once and for all, going to force him to take a side. At lunch, we devised this outlandish story about how we saw a bear running through the middle of downtown, passing cars and running wildly trying to find some wooded area. Everyone in on the hoax had a part. A few friends would argue that it was impossible to have a bear running through the downtown area. A few friends and I took the opposite side of the argument, which it is possible because we saw it happen that afternoon. That evening after practice we were following our ritual of making noodles (you know they cheap ones with packet flavoring) when we started the debate. If I remember correctly, it started off in a mild manner when one of my friends on my side of the argument said, "Guess what we saw today?" After we told the story of what happened, everyone went into character and the debate took off and we were all on the top of our game. Voices were raised, names were probably called and amazingly enough our buddy just sat there watching the television, not saying a word as usual. So we asked him what he thought. Is it possible or not? True to form, he came back with an answer right down the middle of the road. He said something like: "Maybe, it's highly unlikely, but it's possible that it could happen."

Throughout the entire debate, we could never get him to take a stance. He is a dear friend and a man I admire. Fortunately, since those days in college he has changed and now that he has a child of his own he does take stances on issues and is vocal about what he believes.

My friend's opinion (or lack of it) about the bear story is an example of what I see happening in society today. I look at individuals that I work closely with and in a lot of cases I cannot figure out what exactly they believe in or what they stand for. If they do stand for something, then it is not shown through their actions because their actions are constantly changing. In today's world, we are faced with peer pressure like never before and that messes with our moral compass. One day we believe a certain behavior is wrong when we are in the comforts of our family or church groups, and then the next day we find ourselves in the middle of that exact behavior because of outside pressures. Today's society breeds change. It's a society where one day it is cool and then the next day it is not. If you need examples then look at fashion, technology, or other materialistic things. What is "in" today will be obsolete tomorrow. Do you know what never changes or goes out of style? God and His word! What was important hundreds of years ago is important today and will be hundreds of years from now. Biblical morals, character, and values never change and should always be the cornerstones of who we are as individuals.

I cannot tell you what to believe in or force you to believe in anything, but I can give you advice. My advice is that you had better believe in something (hopefully the right things), because if you don't, you will be lost in the shuffle. Too many times we feel as if we will gain respect by doing what others do. We feel that if we are just part of the crowd and tag along, then we will fit in. I hate to burst bubbles here, but that is far from the truth. Some of the people I respect most are people who have opposite beliefs than I do regarding certain topics. I respect them because I admire how they stand up for what they believe in and have the courage to put it on display. Why do I respect that? Because it's so unique nowadays to see consistent actions and beliefs.

God did not put us on this earth with set beliefs. As I said earlier, He gave us the greatest power of all: the power to choose. You have the power to choose what you believe in. He wants us to believe in Him, not because He chooses that for us but rather because it is our choice to believe in Him and follow His word. All the things we have discussed in this book mean nothing if you choose to not believe in yourself and use your platform to make sure that people know exactly what you stand for and believe. Don't waiver or compromise your beliefs. Jesus didn't, as Hebrews 13:8 tells us…

"Jesus Christ is the same yesterday and today and forever."

Stand Up

One might think that having the power to stand up for what he or she believes is derived from courage, but I disagree. I believe that courage comes into play way before that step takes place. I would argue that it takes courage to not waiver from what you actually believe in, to not follow the crowd and do what's cool today. Standing up for your beliefs is a by-product of the example that you set and action you take when you find yourself staying true to your convictions. It takes courage to be convicted in your beliefs, although we all should be. Matthew 12:36 touches on this…

"But I tell you that everyone will have to give account on the day of judgment for every empty word they have spoken."

The Stay Tru translation of that verse goes like this. On the day of judgment, people will have to account for every time they spoke words or displayed actions that they knew were wrong and not true to what they believed. Or to simplify it, people will have to account for the times they didn't stand up for what they knew was right. Sometimes standing up for something you believe in is easier when we are in the presence of others who share the same beliefs.

Do you know what athletics, competitiveness and taking a stand have in common? To make it to the highest level of athletics, to be the very best at what you do, you will come to realize that taking a stand and working hard is most difficult when **no one** is around. The athlete that succeeds is the athlete that puts in all the hours of hard work, blood, sweat and tears when no one is watching. There is **no one** there patting them on the back or screaming their name. It is just them and they are all alone working to hone their skills to be the very best that they can be. The reward is when they get to compete in front of an audience. That is their platform. For us, the same rings true. It is most difficult to stand up for what you believe in when **no one** is watching, holding you accountable. When you are all alone, just know, that those are the times that you need to be practicing, honing your skills to do what is right, staying true to your beliefs. If you can realize and understand that concept then you will not need courage when you find yourself on your platform, in front of an audience standing up for what you truly believe. Your natural abilities that you have been practicing over and over will automatically shine through.

Step Out

A point that I am always trying to get across to people I work with is that they are going to have to, at some point, step outside of their comfort zone. In chapter seven we talked about change and how we get comfortable and dislike a change to our routine. This is the "*if it isn't broke then don't fix it*" mentality. Well, we do need to change, and when it comes to believing in yourself, there is no better way to solidify what you believe in than to take a step out of your comfort zone.

To me it is like a final exam. Imagine going to class and doing homework (finding out what you truly believe in and what you have a passion for), then taking some tests (being able to stand up when no one is around, having the self-discipline to do what is right, control your attitude and effort) and then finally at the end of the semester you will have to take the final exam. The final exam is this: stepping outside of your comfort zone. It is easy to get excited about a particular sport or hobby when you find yourself surrounded by people who share the same passion. The true test comes when you find yourself on an island, when you are in an environment that you are not used to and surrounded by unfamiliar faces. I explain it to individuals I mentor this way:

Think about the last time you found yourself acting goofy and letting loose. I would guess that in those moments you were in a comfortable situation surrounded by family or friends. Now think about that behavior and tell me if you would act the same way if you were surrounded by a group of people that you had never met before - a group that consisted of total strangers who came from different backgrounds or cultures. I would guess that the answer would be no, unless you have an amazingly outgoing personality. If my guess is correct, then allow me to add this: We as human beings find it easier to stay true to who we are and follow our beliefs when we are in a safe, comfortable environment. When we find ourselves surrounded by individuals that may not share the same beliefs as we do, then we would tag that as an unsafe or uncomfortable environment.

The generation of young adults coming up often find themselves going back and forth between these two environments. They find it easy to give 100% in practice when others around them are giving the same amount of effort. Why? Because they do not want to be left behind, they want to keep pace. It is easy for them to express their faith and have a good heart when they are in a safe environment, such as church or youth groups, but find it difficult to express the same passion when they find themselves in an unsafe environment such as a high school party or a team bus ride where others around them are expressing thoughts and beliefs that contradict their own. Standing up and stepping out are some of the hardest things that we may do in our lives. It is not easy to live a fruitful life, one that exemplifies a true follower of Christ and not just a fan of Christ. If we believe that nothing in life that is worthwhile comes easily, then magnify that and understand that following Christ may be one of the toughest things you will have to do on earth. Also understand it will be the most rewarding.

Stay Tru, stand up for yourself and do not be afraid to step outside of your comfort zone for what you believe in. That is what a true leader is all about, that is what earns respect and admiration from others. Do not blend in; be different. I dare you.

Shine

The last "S" and the most rewarding of them all is *shine*. If you have strong convictions to stand up and step out, then go ahead and let your bright light shine! I don't mean in a cocky way, like *hey look at me,* but rather in a happy way. You should feel good if you are at a point in your life where you know what it is you stand, and have a passion, for. Express that passion! You don't need to go out and buy a megaphone and start yelling at the top of your lungs, you just need to show up and be confident in what your light stands for. If you don't have the confidence in what you stand for, then trust me, others around you will recognize that. Two verses I refer to when it comes to this topic are Matthew 5:16 and Daniel 12:3:

"In the same way, let your light shine before me, that they

may see your good deeds and praise your Father in heaven."

"Those who are wise will shine like the brightness of the heavens, and those who lead many to righteousness, like the stars for ever and ever."

Remember in chapter three when I asked you to rank what is most important to you and your family, and what consumes most of your thoughts and attention? Well, if you have come to a point in your life where your lists align (maybe not perfectly but your top two should be the same in each list), then it is imperative that you shine your light for others to see. I need you to shine your light. The world needs you to step out and shine your light. Why is it so important? If we choose to not step up and shine, then we will not be setting an example through our actions and beliefs. The consequences of such decisions can be long lasting. We would allow negative examples and darkness to take over in group situations.

Have you ever been to a party or a get-together with friends and you did not like the path the situation was taking? In those moments, what did you do? Did you choose to blend in and just get through the evening or did you take a stand for what you believe in and excuse yourself from the situation? You may think that excusing yourself from the situation is giving up, but I disagree. Excusing yourself shows others that you stand for something different and that you are more concerned with your beliefs than you are your popularity. I think a class should be taught on how to stand up and excuse yourself from events that you find uncomfortable. Sometimes stepping up and saying nothing sends a message louder than any words ever could.

I had a friend who was a professional athlete. He was asked to be a part of a promotion for a local company. A few days after agreeing to do the promotion, he learned that some of the events that were going to take place did not align with his beliefs. Upon learning this, he didn't stand up and yell at anyone. He didn't say anything negative about what they were doing. He called the company and told them that he appreciated the fact that they thought of him for the event, but he had to respectfully decline. When they asked why, he responded politely and told them he felt that some of the events that were to take place would compromise what he stood for and he was not comfortable being a part of it. I can tell you, his response sent a far louder message than if he had walked into their offices and started screaming. The way he handled himself and how he stayed true to his beliefs sent a powerful message. After the fact, when I talked to him about it, he told me something I will never forget: "There are consequences if we choose to not stand up for what we believe in." We never really went into more detail, so I was left to ponder what he said and think about what it meant.

Remember the saying that goes something like…
"Bad things happen when good people do nothing".

That saying sums up your light and the answer to what my friend told me that day we talked. If you are a person who has the tools that we have discussed in this book, then I need you to shine. Correct that, **the world** needs you. We need everyone to step out and let their light shine because if we do not, then those out there trying to use their platforms, in the right way, will be overpowered by the darkness that surrounds them. We have to work together.

I urge you not to fall into the trap of letting your light flicker due to fear or confusion. If you have strong beliefs and stand up for what you believe in but do not express confidence or happiness, then others will notice. They will feel like you are not quite sure you actually believe in what you say or do. Do not be that person. Do not be afraid to be different. I think you will find that there are many individuals among you that feel as you feel, think as you think, and dare to be different as you do, but they need a leader to guide them (This will be discussed in the next chapter). I sometimes give individuals I work closely with this poem I wrote:

> You are doing the work, you are paying the price
> You might not be as popular but you are twice as nice
>
> Do not worry about your legacy or fate
> Your example brings envy from others looking to find their clean slate
>
> So go out and let others experience your happiness and bright light
> Let it shine through the darkest of nights
>
> For you are not perfect by any means
> But you have a heart that believes
>
> So do not give up and stand alone
> Many are with you, waiting to join and reap what they have sown
>
> So when all of your bright lights shine as one
> You can take pride in knowing that your legacy has just begun

Parents, Coaches, Mentors

This is going to be short and sweet. As people of influence, it is important for us to realize that we have to instill the blueprint of self-belief into those we care about. If an individual cannot find the motivation and desire to do what is right when no one is looking, then they definitely will not be able to constantly do what is right when they are on display (on their platform). Sure, they may be able to fake it or hide it for a little while but eventually their true colors will shine. If they cannot find the motivation to give 100% in practice then they will find times where they are not giving 100% in game-type situations. That may be OK when we are talking about certain athletic fields of competition but what happens when they are in the game of life? What happens when their habits start carrying over from their hobbies and pastimes to their everyday life? When we are in a position of influence, we have a responsibility to make sure that those we care about have the self-belief and tools available to them that will allow them to stand up, step out and shine. Lou Holtz mentioned he lives by three rules and, when he was a football coach, he instilled these three rules into his teams:

1) Do what is right. If you don't know what is right then get out your Bible.
2) Do your very best at all times.
3) Treat others the way you want to be treated.

There is not one basic blueprint out there that outlines the exact keys to instilling certain behaviors and traits into those we care about. However, there are reference manuals that can steer you in the right direction (how about this book?) Of course, the first and last reference should be the Bible. If I could add a fourth to Lou's three rules, it would be:

4) Give others the encouragement and self-belief to stand up, step out and shine.

I believe, wholeheartedly, that once an individual has the ability to let their light shine then they will have the ability to impact others and become a leader that we are so desperately missing. Have you ever wondered why it is unique to see people with large platforms act the right way and do the right things? Have you ever sat back and thought to yourself that an individual may seem too good to be true? Then when you see them using their platform in such a positive way you pray that it is the real deal and not just a show? Why do you think we ask those questions? We, as a whole, have lost the ability to hope, dream and stand up for what we truly believe. We have lost the passion, at times, to be unpopular and go against what is normal and let our light shine. This may not be true all of the time, but it has happened to all of us at some point. Sure, we have no problem voicing our opinion but that's not what is important. What is important is that we rediscover the passion within to become a playmaker for what we believe through our actions and the way we carry ourselves. We desperately need playmakers!

Tasks

1) What is it that you believe in?
2) Have you ever stood up, stepped out and shined for what you believe in? If so, explain the situation.
3) Do you encourage others around you to shine? If so, who and give an example.
4) Do you find your light flickering at times? If so, explain how you re-ignite your flame.
5) Come up with and write down three rules that you need to follow in order for your light to shine the brightest.

Chapter 10

Become a Playmaker

We are nearing the end of the circle that I have referred to throughout this book. I do believe that everything is tied together and works as a unit. It is like a fine-tuned team. A great team has a little of everything: a competitive spirit, a willingness to sacrifice, dares to be different, a passionate person, a belief in itself and playmakers. But in faith, sacrifice means that in order to go to heaven you must first die.

In sports, every team needs a playmaker. It needs that one person that leads others and makes things happen. In athletics, a playmaker keeps the team cool when things are not going so well. When the opposite occurs and a team has success, the playmaker keeps his or her teammates humble. A playmaker is the coach out on the floor; all instruction goes through the playmaker because the coach and team trusts them to be a leader, through action and example. The sporting world has playmakers. We need to take a page out of that playbook and learn how to become a playmaker in life.

So what is a playmaker? The Merriam-Webster online dictionary says (I love throwing out definitions because I like to feel smart, and I learn a lot about myself in the process) that a playmaker is:

> "A player who leads the offense for a team"

I love that definition and the way we can break it down. To do that, I am going to re-word it and give you the Stay Tru definition.

"A playmaker is an individual that takes the initiative to lead other individuals or a team."

The key words that I changed were…"player" to "individual", "offense" to "initiative" and "team" to "other individuals or a team". Why did I do that? Because in life we need playmakers but we are not players in a game, we are individuals trying to make a difference. Let's break it down according to the changes I made to the definition…

Player to Individual

We may not all be a part of some athletic team, but we all have a team. Your team may be your family, it may be your spouse, or your spouse and children. Your team could be your co-workers or maybe it is your Bible study group. No matter what team you are a part of, it is important that each team has a playmaker. When trying to become a playmaker in life we may need a little encouragement or guidance at times. I know I do and I have come across this verse that helps. Colossians 3:23:

> *"Whatever you do, work at it with all your heart, as working for the Lord, not for human masters."*

A playmaker in life does not have a scoreboard that tells us whether we are winning or losing. There is no scorecard we can write a number on and others are not judging us on a scale of 1-10. It would be a lot easier if that were the case, right? Just imagine if we each had our own individual scoreboard that we carried with us. Whenever we did anything good, God would change the score and add a point to our total. The opposite would be true as well. If we did something we were not supposed to, God would add points onto the other team's score. How great would that be? To be able to look at the scoreboard and see exactly where we stood; to see if we were winning or losing. If things were getting a little out of hand we could call a timeout and regroup. Or, if we were on a roll we could just keep going full steam ahead and ride out our scoring streak for as long as possible. Nice thought, right? Well, it is not that easy and we do not have a scoreboard. Worse than that, God has given us the inevitable task of judging ourselves.

The Colossians 3:23 verse points out the fact that we do have to judge ourselves. In that process we are judged by one question. When we do something, are we giving our very best and doing it for the Lord? If the answer is yes, then one point for you. If the answer is no, then one point goes to the other team. The more times we can give ourselves a point, the closer we are to becoming a playmaker.

If God is our coach and the Bible is our playbook, then our goal should be to become His floor general in the world today. We should be His light that shines bright. David Platt wrote a book titled "Follow Me". In that book, David touched on how we should approach each day as if we were walking out into the mission field. No matter where we are at on a particular day, or who we come into contact with, we should always have the mindset of serving and helping others. I may not be explaining it correctly word for word but I completely agree with what David was trying to express. We need to wake up each day and be playmakers for all those we come into contact with. We should be the person that keeps everyone on the same page and makes sure the team and those around us are primed for success. A playmaker in life makes sure the team is giving 100% in practice and preparing in the right ways. When game day comes the team will look to their playmaker to lead whether times are good or times are bad. When we get knocked down our playmaker will be there to help us get up and keep pushing ahead.

We all have the ability to become a playmaker, to be that one individual that leads others. It is not easy, but then again what that is worthwhile is?

Offense to Initiative

The word ***offense***, for our purposes, (again from the Merriam-Webster online dictionary) means…

"The means or method of attacking or attempting to score"

Focus on the word ***attack***. The definition of playmaker does not include the word defense; it uses the word offense, which means attack or score. It is imperative that if we want to become a playmaker in life we need to attack situations, not play defense against them.

Have you ever watched a sporting event where it seemed a team or individual was always on the attack and the only thing their opponent could do was try to play defense as best as they possibly could? In sports, we call that ***a lopsided affair***. In this situation, an opponent is overmatched and has no ability to win no matter what they do. I have seen that example play out in sports time and time again, as I have in life.

If we are going to become true playmakers, we first have to make a commitment to give 100% and do all things with the right intentions. Secondly, we have to take the initiative to be offensive and tackle situations head on, not sit back and wait for them to attack us. If we allow things to attack us then we will consistently find ourselves on defense, and that is not what a playmaker does. Constantly playing defense will fatigue you to the point where you want to give up. I love using this example. When I watch a basketball game it always cracks me up to watch certain players. In the course of a game when the action goes back and forth, you will start to see players fatigued and tired. They start grabbing onto their shorts and breathing heavily. As interesting as that may be, what fascinates me is that you mostly see those examples on the defensive side of the court. You will see players not moving as fast, a little slower and their defense shows it. However, when they get to the offensive end of the court they all of sudden have some unknown burst of energy, especially if they have the ball in their hand. Why is that? It is simple. It is a lot more fun to play offense in any game than it is to play defense. My late Uncle Steve would say to me, "How many times do you read a headline in the newspaper where it mentions how good a player played on defense? It doesn't. Now, tell me how many times the headline tells you how many points a player scored to lead his team to victory? All the time." He would also tell me that when I was hot I should keep shooting, and when I wasn't hot to keep shooting until I got hot. But that is for another book. Do you get the point I am trying to make? In our society, we pay tribute to offense because it is more rewarding than playing defense. So, if that is true then it should be easy to be on offense, right? Not particularly.

Offense, like anything, is a trait that has to be learned. We have to learn how to be offensive-minded and take initiative. Sometimes in life we are used to sitting back and reacting to what happens instead of being proactive in making sure something does not happen. How many times have you seen something and said to yourself, "That thing is going to break" or "I need to take care of xyz", only to put it off until something happens and then you are forced to take care of the problem at hand? I would say a lot of times in life that happens to us. We need to make sure that when it comes to the important areas of life we become proactive. If we see areas of our life that need fixed then we need to be a play-maker and take the initiative to fix them immediately. If we sit back and wait, we will find ourselves in a lopsided affair. No matter how good of defense we play, at the end of the day we will be chalking up a point for the other team.

Team to Individuals or Part of a Team

Jesus didn't immediately go out to a group and ask them to follow Him. Jesus went to an individual, then another and another and asked them individually to follow Him, to be His disciples. I think He did that because He knew it would be easier to spread His word through a team rather than through large groups. He did that because He knew the importance of having a group of individuals that could be there for one another. He knew that some days His disciples would need each other to lean on, to pick up the slack when one was troubled or falling behind. Lastly, He knew a team was much stronger than one individual standing alone.

Your team is made up of individuals that all have different strengths and weaknesses. They all bring a different trait to the table therefore you have to treat each individual differently. If you treated each one in the exact same manner then you would find yourself communicating effectively with some but not so effectively with others. We all have different struggles in our life and need different tools that will help us turn our weaknesses into strengths. Imagine that I am a gopher boy on a job site working with a group of carpenters. They are building a garage and since they are all up on ladders, they look to me to bring them the proper tools they need at a particular time. If one carpenter was nailing the beams in place, then he would look for me to bring him a hammer. If the carpenter next to him was cutting off the excess wood, then he would need me to bring him a saw. It wouldn't make sense if I brought them the exact same tools and said, "There ya go, good luck, holler when you're done." They would look at me like I was crazy and I imagine I wouldn't have a job for very long. Even though they are a team of carpenters, all trained in the same profession, their needs are all different. Their needs change depending on what stage of the project they are on, or what task they are handling at that moment. It is the same for us playmakers when we are dealing with our team. Our job is to lead. Do you know how to lead most effectively? (hint, I mentioned it earlier) You lead effectively by serving. When you are the playmaker you serve those on your team. You are their gopher boy, running around making sure they have the exact tools they need to fix the project they are working on, which will allow them to succeed and finish their task.

A big obstacle we face is that we do not take the time to understand each team member's individual needs. How can we give someone we care about the proper tools if we do not know what part of life's project they are working on? I urge you to go out and talk to your teammates. Ask them what struggles they are facing in their lives. Let them know that you are there, and that you will make sure they have the proper tools in their hands. You will see personalities shine when they realize that you are there to serve and help them, rather than dictate to them. However, being a playmaker and helping individuals is not doing the work for them. The definition tells us we are to lead, not do.

Parents, Coaches, Mentors

This has been one of the more enjoyable chapters for me to write because it is something that I struggle with every day. At times I find it easy to be a playmaker, while other times I find myself going through the motions and basically taking a day off. I often see things that need fixed when training athletes, whether it is their attitude, effort or focus, but I sometimes choose to ignore them. I find that I am playing defense some days a lot more than I am playing offense. I tell myself that I will attempt to play offense and address those issues some other day when I have more energy to do so. Can you relate?

As a parent or mentor, we have to wake up every day and give ourselves whatever pep talk we deem necessary in order to make sure we start the day off as a playmaker. You can be assured that something will always happen where you will be looked at for guidance and support. You may find that you need to take a few moments to re-energize yourself so that you can continue being the playmaker that your team needs. It won't always be easy, but we need to find a good balance.

It is important that those we influence see us living out what we are trying to express. If we ever needed to be reminded of that it is now, in this chapter, covering these topics of being a playmaker. Those we lead watch our actions closely. Believe me when I say that there is a big difference between playing offense and defense in life. It will be very noticeable to those watching so we have to be on our "A" game at all times. If we are not, and find ourselves playing defense, then it sends mixed messages that lead to future problems.

When I am having one of those days where my mind is in the "fix it later" mode, I try hard to just step away for a few moments and regroup. If I do not do that then I will continue to allow something that I know is wrong to go on. When someone does something over and over, whether it is right or wrong, it creates habits. If I choose to ignore something then I am allowing a bad habit to get worse. When I am finally having an offensive day and I try to be proactive and tackle the bad habits head on, I find myself facing a much bigger issue than a bad habit. I find myself tackling a bad habit and a confused individual. Usually I have to explain to the person who I am working with that the way they were doing things the other day was wrong as well; however, I just must not have caught it. That phrase "I just must not have caught it" is code for "I was too lazy to point it out and I am sorry."

It is the whole fix-it-now or fix-it-later debate. When you see issues on your team, I can promise you that you will have to deal with and fix them at some point. The longer you wait to fix a little issue, the bigger the issue becomes. We are not perfect; we all have our off days and go through our slumps. However, if you do your best to be consistent, to be a playmaker and be on the offensive then you will find out quickly that your off days are not so bad. Why? Because you will have been a leader by example and when you fall, a teammate will come forward and pick up the slack. That is what I call a successful team; when others can look you in the eye on a bad day and tell you not to worry because they are there for you and they have your back. When there is that kind of emotion, then the team you are a part of will become successful. Not just one of you will be successful, you all will be successful. Teams in disarray are always on the defensive because when something goes wrong they are always pointing fingers, never stepping up to take the load off another individual. They are more concerned with their progress and success than that of their team. Create a successful team. Be an individual that takes initiative and attacks problems when they arise, don't sit back and wait until it is too late. Once you have found that balance, teach others how to do the same.

Tasks

1) Do you find yourself being more offensive or defensive in life?
2) Explain a situation where you saw a problem with someone close to you and you took the initiative to help them fix it.
3) Write down three to five obstacles you have in life that you are trying to overcome.
4) Write down the tools you need in order to overcome those obstacles.
5) Are you a playmaker or do you know who the playmaker on your team is?
6) Write down a few sentences on what you feel you could do in order to become a playmaker for your team if you are not, or a better one if you feel you already are.

Chapter 11

Top 1%

Remember the movie ***Top Gun***? When my family finally got surroundsound in our home, we went out and bought that movie to test out the new system. We cranked the volume up loud, popped a few bags of popcorn, and all sat back and listened to the jet engines roar with huge smiles on our faces. That movie was inspiring to me; it gave me the chills and triggered my imagination. I mean, how couldn't it, a jet fighter-pilot movie that showcases the best of the best, competing for the top prize of being recognized as the top pilot in the Navy. I remember years later when I was hitting my competitive stride, I would invite my friends and teammates over and we would watch that movie and talk about how we were the basketball version of ***Top Gun***, the best of the best (during that time you wouldn't believe how many summer league teams named themselves "Top Gun").

I refer to that movie a lot when I am pondering things in my life or trying to motivate individuals to work hard, pursue their dreams and become the best they can possibly be. I tell them to go home and watch it, come back and let me know how the movie made them feel. It is funny because when the men watch it, they come back all pumped up and inspired. They talk about how cool the movie was and how motivated they are to become the best. When the women watch it, they come back and tell me how sad the movie was because Goose dies and they talk about how they cried. I now advise people who are going to watch the movie to focus on the story it tells and its motivating aspects rather than the sad parts. If they follow my advice, they will watch a movie that shows individuals at the top of their profession competing for an ultimate prize. They will see an individual full of confidence broken down to his core and his process of finding the motivation to return to the top. They will see adversity and obstacles being overcome by the power of belief that our teammates and mentors have in us. The movie has many deeper messages that go beyond the cool air scenes and loud jet engines but we will come back to that.

At some point in our lives, we will find ourselves giving everything we have to be the very best that we can be at a particular pursuit that has captured our attention and passion. The activity will vary, but be assured you will find yourself spending countless hours and dollars trying to become better. Where does that come from? Why do certain activities capture our attention and imagination so much?

Do you know any individual that takes up a sport or hobby and becomes borderline obsessed? I have friends that play golf, hunt, fish or ski. I have watched them spend countless hours practicing on the driving range or scouting the land. I have seen them spend thousands and thousands of dollars buying new equipment, taking lessons to improve their technique or buying the latest clothing and gimmicks. I wish I could say that I just had friends that I saw these traits in, but that would not be the truth. I, too, have fallen under this spell. I am competitive by nature; I just love the thrill of competition. I have picked up certain hobbies through the years and become so focused on becoming good at them that it could be classified as borderline obsessive. I am sure as you read this you can relate due to personal experiences or you may know someone that fits this description.

There is nothing wrong in striving to be the best you can possibly be at a particular activity. I think it is healthy to have passion, but I also think we need to ask ourselves where that passion comes from and why we are willing to sacrifice so much time and money on certain activities that in the end give us no reward. As we ask that question we also need to look at why we choose to spend a fraction of our energy on things that, when all is said and done, can give us a huge payoff. Again, look at the question, "Why do people do what they do?" Let's take that a step further here and ask why do they choose to devote so much time in the wrong places? Could it be because they are confused?

Yes, people are confused in life. Very recently, I had a conversation with an athlete I train. One of the individuals, who we will name Kim, was pressing way too hard and that was causing her to make mistake after mistake. What I saw happening to Kim was not unusual. It happens to all of us when we make mistakes – we tend to lose our confidence and the more we fail the harder we press which usually makes things worse. Well, Kim's confidence was shot and I was trying to figure out why. It only took two questions on my part before the tears started to flow. I asked, "Why is it so important to you that you are good at your sport? Why do you compete?" Her response was, "It is what I am known for and it is why people like me." That answer led to a much longer conversation than I had anticipated, and I could go on and on about it, but the point is, her love for a sport had been replaced with a growing desire to excel so that she could feel accepted and make others around her happy. She was in a place where she wanted to be the best at something for all the wrong reasons. I am not saying that Kim doesn't love to compete, but at this point in her life she was competing so that she could find her identity instead of playing for the pure love and passion she once had. Her platform was in shambles and so the rebuilding process had to begin. You could say she needed a playmaker to help guide her through the obstacle before her.

The place Kim found herself in and her thought process is a common one. We often lose sight of the reasons that once motivated us to compete or be the best we could be. We start to focus on the distractions around us and become more concerned with pleasing those little things, which have no substantial long-term meaning or benefit, than pleasing ourselves. It is true when it comes to our faith as well. We will find times in our life where we will lose our passion and succumb to the desires of feeling accepted and pleasing others rather than making sure our inner desires fuel our actions and motives. Jesus knew we would fall into this rut, and be weak in mind and spirit, so the Bible gives us references to help steer us back onto the proper path.

2 Corinthians 12:9: But he said to me "My grace is sufficient for you, for my power is made perfect in weakness." Therefore I will boast all the more gladly about my weaknesses, so that Christ's power may rest on me.

In this verse, Paul is pointing out that being weak does not mean we are lost or broken. Rather, admitting weaknesses shows our strength and ability to grow by the understanding that through God all things are possible and that yes, we do need His help.

The conversation I had with Kim that day was one of many. I tried to help Kim understand the importance of admitting her weaknesses, as we all have them, and using her faith as a fuel to find strength and joy in taking advantage of the talents and abilities she has been blessed with. I shared with her my weaknesses and times I found myself doing things for the wrong reasons. I promised her that if we focused on doing our best and giving thanks and glory to God then we would be blessed no matter what outcome we had in competition. I explained to her that, in life, there are contenders and pretenders. We vowed to help one another become a contender.

Contender or Pretender?

I read a book not long ago titled **Not a Fan** by a pastor in Louisville, KY, whose name is Kyle Idleman. It is a great book and one I highly recommend you read. In his book, Kyle talks about what it means to be a follower of Jesus Christ and not just a fan of Jesus Christ (hence the reason I kept thinking in my mind the phrase contender or pretender). Kyle does an amazing job pointing out the difference between being a fan and a true follower. As I was reading his book, I immediately started to think about what we choose to be a fan of and why, and what we choose to be a follower of and why. I was trying to relate it to my life and my experiences. I know that the book was specifically relating to our relationship with Jesus Christ but I was thinking about all of the other areas of life.

In my life I see both contenders and pretenders. I see many pretenders who wish they were contenders, but they do not know what that truly means – that it takes being the best of the best. They do not know how to strive to be in the top 1%. Some individuals may know the sacrifice that it takes to be the very best, but they lose the drive and motivation to make that dream become a reality. I am not just talking about our relationship with Jesus Christ. I am talking about our everyday lives and what we are passionate about. I am talking about what consumes our time and efforts and what we find ourselves spending so much energy and money on.

When it comes to the examples I witness every day, I see people that put a lot of time and effort into causes that are meaningless in the end. I see people like Kim who are emotionally exhausted because they have wasted so much energy holding on too tight. They want success so badly because they feel if they don't attain it they will lose their identity. The Bible has many references to being a pretender and how it affects ones identity. Proverbs 13:7 and Proverbs 12:9 state:

> *"One person pretends to be rich, yet has nothing; another pretends to be poor, yet has great wealth."*
>
> *"Better to be a nobody and yet have a servant than pretend to be somebody and have no food."*

There comes a point where we need to sit back and determine what is important to us, what we desire, and make sure we are using our resources efficiently. We have to make the choice and decide if we are going to be a contender or a pretender. A contender is strong, confident and isn't in it for the fame or recognition. A contender works hard and is successful because they dare to be different and have self-belief and know that it takes hard work and commitment to be in the top 1%. A pretender on the other hand is someone that is focused on all of the wrong things. Their light will fizzle out because when things start going sideways they have no self-belief to fall back on. Do you know what happens when you tell yourself not to do something? A lot of times you end up doing it. That's what a pretender does. Instead of being grateful for what talents they do have and dreaming about what they can do with them they choose to focus on what they don't have, what they are not doing, or what they cannot do. A pretender will start to panic because their identity, in their minds, may be lost.

How do you tell the difference between a contender and a pretender? There may be a few answers that I could give but the most important one you need to understand deals with comparison. Contenders understand that they might be a little different or unique. They do not see that as a fault but rather it serves as their motivation. Life is not a popularity contest for them, rather their popularity is self-measured through their personal relationship with God and the understanding of what motivates their actions. Pretenders, on the other hand, get caught up in comparisons. They look at other athletes that are better than they are and immediately start to compare themselves, wondering why they are not as good, can't jump as high or don't have the same successes (Note: It is not wrong to look at others that we admire and look at things they do well then use that as a learning experience for self-improvement). The same holds true in school, place of employment, and within family and friends. Where do you think the mentality "the grass is greener" comes from? Pretenders see something that looks better, compares it to their current situation and thinks "Hey, they have it a lot better than I do. I want to be like them, or have what they have." If you have the mentality where you find yourself always comparing your life or situations to others then you are pretending (much different than dreaming). Maybe you know people around you that are pretenders. If so, I encourage you to use your platform and have a talk with them, explaining the difference between a contender and a pretender.

I know a professional golfer who told me a story his late father shared with him. "Imagine you were in a room full of people and a speaker asked everyone in attendance to take out a piece of paper and pen and write down all of the problems going on in their lives. After everyone finished, the speaker proceeded to tell everyone to take off his or her right shoe and put the paper inside. The speaker then said that they could trade their shoe for another shoe and, if they did, all of their problems would be gone, however, the shoe that they received and the problems inside would now be theirs. Would you trade your shoe for another?"

Everyone has problems. Contenders realize this and are proactive in meeting their issues head on, choosing to deal with them and keep moving forward. A pretender sits back and compares, does nothing but wishes things were different. Worse, they keep doing what they have been doing hoping things will eventually change, which usually does not happen. Scary thought.

I told Kim that we had to get her into a place where she was a contender, not a pretender. Kim had to stop comparing herself to a standard that she felt others had for her. She had to stop pretending and start being the best that she could be, let go and let the pieces fall where they may. More importantly, I tried to help Kim understand the difference between short-term happiness that comes from doing things to please others and long-term happiness that comes from the satisfaction and fulfillment of pleasing God. I feel the same way for all of you reading this book. I do not want you to be average and I definitely do not want you to follow the same examples that I see every day. I have bigger plans for you. I want you to be different and take pride in that. I want you to be a contender, not a person that compares. Lastly, I want you to understand what it takes to be in the top 1% of anything that you do. I don't claim to have all the answers, but I do believe that, in order to become great at anything, you first need to have a sense of resolve. Having calmness within you will allow your abilities to shine. If you are confused about why you are striving to be the best of the best then you will eventually fail because you will hold on way too tight and focus more on the immediate affirmation that you receive from those around you.

The Trap

A while back I was driving down the road to a place I had never been. I was following every direction the GPS gave me, but I found it odd that I was out in the middle of nowhere when I was supposed to be surrounded by the sights of buildings and a vibrant city. Every time I made a turn, the time of arrival to my destination got pushed back by five minutes or so. I started to get upset and knew something had to be terribly wrong but I kept asking myself how could the GPS not be right? It is a computer device that has the map programmed into its system, so how could it lead me in the wrong direction? Finally, after what seemed like an eternity, I passed a small country gas station so I decided to stop and ask for some assistance. I went inside, and luckily there was a man that knew how to get me to where I wanted to go. That was the good news. The bad news was I had traveled 30 minutes out of the way. When he asked how I ended up way out in the country, I told him I was following my GPS. He started laughing; I, on the other hand, was not.

I trusted the GPS to get me to where I wanted to go in a timely manner. It failed me that day. Have you ever felt like you were on the right road in life only to find out that the devices that you trusted had let you down? Have you ever fallen into that trap?

Coming to the conclusion of whether we are a contender or a pretender is half the battle. The other half is determining what devices we are going to use to help us navigate the path that will lead us to our eventual destination.

When I sat down that afternoon and talked to Kim, I can assure you that she thought she was on the right path. She wasn't happy but she felt she was just a little lost and eventually her navigation system would lead her to her ultimate destination. What Kim had to realize was her slump was being caused by false information. That afternoon she had to take the steps to begin the rebuilding process and that meant stopping what she was doing and asking for a new set of directions.

I can relate to her struggles because I have been there many times. I imagine that if you are reading this book, you may be able to as well. We are surrounded by so much information that it is easy to fall into the trap of thinking we are on the right path, only to be disappointed when we realize we are truly lost. So how do we prevent that from happening?

To be the best of the best, we have to take the guesswork out of why we do what we do. We have to know exactly why it is we do certain things and we have to be certain in the tools we use that will help us reach our goals. I recommend that you start by making sure your priorities are in line. You can do a self-check by determining if the things you are devoting time and energy to are the things in your life that you find most important. After you have come to that point in the process you must start probing and planning your roadmap.

Roadmap

A roadmap is an outline of the things that are important to you and the goals you wish to accomplish. Your road map should also include a lot of people you can rely on and people who will hold you accountable along the way. Lastly, you should also list the possible traps that would cause you to take a wrong turn and have a plan to avoid them. When completed, your roadmap should be a life summary and an instruction manual in one. How do you get started in developing a roadmap?

Probe: You first have to ask yourself the questions I just outlined and write out each answer. What is important to you in life? What goals do you wish to accomplish and why? Who are the individuals that will mentor you and hold you accountable? And lastly, what traps do you foresee that may arise?

I recommend that you answer those questions then revisit them in a few days. Have you ever been in a conversation and wanted to tell someone something but you just could not remember what that was? Then as soon as you leave the conversation or the next day you pinch yourself because you finally remembered? It happens all of the time and will happen to you when you are in the middle of this process. So, I advise that you revisit your answers a few days later and add anything you may have forgotten. Once you have studied and answered all of those questions, then you are ready for the next step in the process: planning.

Planning: The key point in this process is that you do not plan alone. You need to grab an individual that you listed as someone you will confide in to mentor, motivate and hold you accountable. Why? Because if they are going to be someone you count on, clear communication must be present at all times. They need to know where your heart is and why you do what you do.

So, once you have that individual identified, the road mapping process can begin. I recommend that you start by outlining your big goals. What do you want years from now? Is it to be a college athlete? Do you want to own your own business? Do you desire to become a better spouse, family member or friend? Whatever it may be, write down the big goals that you want to achieve. Once you have written them down I want you to make a column and title it "Faith." The definition of faith that I have heard and like the most is "believing when there is no reason to." In that column list traits you will need in order to give yourself the best chance to make your goals become a reality. Examples could be attitude, passion, never giving up and so on. After you have outlined a few key traits, I want you to explain how your faith and beliefs will help you succeed. I would urge you also to list some Bible verses related to your outlined traits. It is useful to have them handy so you can use them as reference points whenever you feel like you are starting to slack off. Once you have those tasks completed, it's time to start moving backward. You should start making lists of things you need to do starting now. An example would be if your goal is to become a college athlete then you need to get stronger, quicker and faster. So you would outline a training program that you will follow to help you become all of those things. If it is to become a better spouse or friend then maybe you make a list of traits you feel are holding you back and areas you know you need to see improvement. Those traits could be listening more, taking more of an interest in things that are important to those we care about, etc. Again, write some Bible verses down in the faith column that deal with the topics you wish to improve on. Lastly, and a very key area, you need to make a section of your roadmap that outlines obstacles or traps that you foresee could hinder your growth and keep you from achieving your goals. Usually these things are outside influences such as friends, technology, lack of materials and so on. No one that has ever achieved some form of success did it without overcoming some obstacle. They will always be present. You may not always see them right away but they will surface. The key to overcoming roadblocks is to be proactive, not reactive. As we discussed in the last chapter, if you want to accomplish what is important to you then you need to become a playmaker and make things happen. Making a list of the traps you feel you will face, and a list of the tools you will need to overcome them, will prevent you from being surprised when they occur. It is much easier to handle roadblocks in life when we know they are coming. What is difficult is when we are blindsided with surprises. When that happens we find ourselves scrambling both mentally and physically.

There is no ready-made outline for your roadmap. When I have done this exercise I bought a notebook and titled each page with a question that was listed above. After I spent time answering those questions I would take a sheet and make three columns titled goal, faith, and trap. I would outline my goals and list faith characteristics I need to help me along my journey and then listed traps I felt could get in the way of what I wanted to achieve. Lastly I would start to work backwards and break my larger goals down into more specific mini-goals, again using the three columns. When it was completed I had a list of goals, knew the obstacles I would face, spiritual references that I could go back to for motivation and a list of individuals that I knew were on my team, and this roadmap would help me become successful.

Parents, Coaches, Mentors

As I said early in this chapter, the movie *Top Gun* excites and motivates many. It is easy to sit back, watch that movie and dream of being great. It captures our imagination because it looks fun and thrilling. We know that if we were ever in a fighter jet we would experience emotions that we have never felt before. Maybe that is what triggers our imagination. I have come to learn that the things in life that give us immediate thrill and satisfaction are things that will leave us empty in the end. However, the things that may be difficult to get excited about each and every day are the very things that will give us the greatest thrill we could ever receive. It is hard to imagine life after death. When we talk about it I am sure your senses do not cause your hair to stand up on the back of your neck. But, if you dedicate your life to becoming the best of the best, to be the top 1% when it comes to matters of faith, standing up, stepping out and shining on your platform, then

I can comfortably say that when it is all said and done and you cross that finish line you will experience a thrill that no fighter jet could ever give you. We are already in the midst of the game we play each morning we wake up. Let's make the choice to start over today, to be different. Let's finish the game strong.

Once you have all of the tools in place it is up to you to become a playmaker and pass that knowledge to those on your team. As you go through the steps, I think you will realize that your team will get bigger and bigger and your once small platform will be gaining more of an audience. I have started the process of implementing each one of these steps outlined in this book into my daily life. It is not that I didn't know these steps years ago, I just chose not to implement them. Why? Because I thought I was already on the right path, that my navigation system had me heading in a fairly good direction. I was not perfect and I made many mistakes but I would quickly brush them off, as if it was someone else's fault, not mine. As I said earlier, the inspiration for this book came from a tragic loss, the passing of my sister. At that time I chose to look at my life. I knew I had to truly understand what I did and why I did it. That was my first baby step and each day after I have tried to grow and pass on these principles to the athletes I work with. I hope this book allows you to start taking your first steps and fills you with some knowledge that you can pass on to those you care about. Please don't let it take a tragic loss or event in your life before you decide you need to start asking questions. There is an amazing thrill out there waiting for you; it's up to you to get in the race and run. I cannot promise you will be the first to cross the finish line, but that is not what is important. What is important is that you run the race the right way, for the right reasons. Today could be your first day of becoming the best of the best, the top 1%. Go for it!

Tasks

1) What motivates you to the best of the best?
2) Have you ever felt like you were a contender, only to find out you were pretending? If so, explain.
3) Do you see examples in your life of pretenders? If so, what examples do you see?
4) Have you ever thought you were on the right path, only to find out that you were actually lost? If so, explain the situation and the steps you took to get back on the right path.
5) Create your own roadmap and/or help others around you to do the same.

Chapter 12

Finishing the Right Way

Remember chapter five, when I talked about daring to be different? The second dare I threw out was to give a little more than you are used to giving. We can look at that a different way and focus on finishing strong. We may think finishing would come naturally. Logic tells us that if you start something then at some point you must stop and finish, which is true. However we are not talking about just finishing; we are going to focus on how we can finish strong and the effects that has on our lives.

Have you ever watched a sporting event and noticed that certain competitors seem to get better as the game or contest goes on? Sometimes we will hear announcers say those very words when describing the play of a team or athlete. Have you ever wondered why that is?

When I was a senior in high school, my basketball team had a nickname that the local announcer came up with, "The Cardiac Kids." They called us that because it seemed no matter what, we were always behind at halftime. Looking back, I do not recall too many games that we went into the locker room at halftime with a lead. That being said, we did come back and win the majority of our games that season, one time down as many as 21 points in the fourth quarter only to come back and win (hence cardiac kids because we would give our fans the most stressful experiences when they would come watch us play). I cannot explain exactly why we always found ourselves trailing at halftime, but I can explain why we were able to come back and win.

Let's look back at the things we have talked about in recent chapters. I have tried to stress the importance of having passion, believing in yourself, becoming a playmaker and being the very best that you can be. If you were to tie all of those traits together you would have a very powerful package, a package that would allow you to overcome deficits and be victorious in the end. It would be a stretch to say that one person on my team that season had all of those traits, but I can say that as a team we came together and brought the traits we had as individuals to form one powerful package. We had a self-belief within us that no matter how dire the circumstances may have seemed, if we stuck together, believed in each other and gave 110% we would find a way to win. We would find a way to finish strong and run through the finish line, not just coast through it.

As we have discussed over and over in this book, today's society is different and poses many more challenges than ever before. I have come to take that into account every day, but I also know that the things we have discussed are attainable for each and everyone of us because they are choices, not talents. Finishing strong is no different; it is a choice, and not a talent you are born with. Individuals today have to be reminded of that daily.

When I do the conditioning portions of our sports performance workouts I see numerous examples of individuals not finishing strong. When the athletes are running sprints I see them start off like they are on fire, only to see their speed and enthusiasm slowly fall off until they get to the point where they are crossing the finish line in a brisk walk. The words I am loudly speaking (because I wouldn't yell at kids) during their conditioning is, "make sure you hit every line" and "finish strong, run through the finish line, don't jog through it." I would think that after numerous sessions with the athletes they would get the picture and I wouldn't have to talk so loudly, but that's not the case. The athletes have to be reminded daily until it becomes a natural instinct for them. They have lived their life working hard for a particular task, only to slow down and set their cruise control when they see the end in sight. I have set out to change those habits.

These traits are not isolated just to athletes running sprints. These examples are a metaphor of life. I have seen marriages start off like they are on fire only to see, years later, the momentum and passion slowly fade away till they find themselves walking at a brisk pace. We could throw out examples in the workplace, in school, when it comes to our faith and in church. No matter what the example, we all have moments where we are on fire, giving our complete focus to accomplish a particular goal, only to let the flames slowly fade away. We have to learn how to reprogram ourselves so the everyday habits we have are replaced with instincts that allow us to sprint through the finish line when we see it in sight.

Learning to Finish Strong

As I mentioned, it's a choice. So make the choice to finish strong and let's move on...if only it were that easy!

It seems simple but it's not. The key is this: We must fill ourselves with the fuel that makes that choice become a natural instinct. What is the fuel? The fuel consists of everything we have discussed in this book. Our fuel comes from our competitive spirit and using it in the right ways. It comes from our platform, making sure that we lead others through our example. It comes from having a passion and desire for what is most important to us and never slowing down or taking a day off when trying to fulfill that passion. It comes from not being afraid to stand up, step out and shine. And finally, it comes from not being afraid to be a little different. If you want to be the same and just go with the flow, then this book is not for you. However, if you dare to be a little different, if you dare to step out, you will find yourself running and sprinting through the finish line. Once you cross that line you will look back and see that others were closely following you and picked up their own pace because they didn't want to be left behind. That is how you lead, by example. You cannot make choices for others, only for yourself. If you choose to do all of these things, to let your light shine, then others will have one of two choices. They will either follow you and run at the pace you set or they will choose to be left behind. Do not let their pace dictate yours. If you allow that to happen then you are not doing anything different, you are just fitting in. In athletics, as in life, too many of us are just fitting in, doing what seems normal and allowing all of the influences around us to dictate our pace. If you want to learn how to finish strong in athletics, in your marriage, at your job or in school then you have to be the one that takes control. You have to make a choice to fill your tank with the necessary fuel. A car cannot run without gasoline and you as a person cannot run without passion, desire, faith, self-belief or effort.

This is your life, please choose to take control and set the pace for others. Be a Leader!

Where is the Finish Line?

What is your finish line? Where and how do we see the finish line? I have asked myself these questions many times over the past few months. I wonder when enough is enough and when we can finally sit back, relax and say to ourselves, "Job well done." If I work with an athlete and they win three tournaments in a row, have we reached the finish line? If I am working with an individual and they seem to have all of their priorities in the right place, can I then say, "Great job, you have crossed the finish line?" The answer is no. I have been reading this verse a lot lately, and probably should every morning. Proverbs 13:4

> *"A sluggard's appetite is never filled, but the desires of the diligent are fully satisfied."*

We cannot sit back and do nothing and hope for good things to happen. We have to make things happen (be a playmaker). When we become a playmaker, and have some success, we cannot sit back and rest on our accomplishments. We need to keep pushing forward with the same passion and desire, if not more. God did not put us here to rest and become content (if you don't believe me I challenge you to read the book of Job). He put us here to understand we are part of a process and along the way we will have some failures and some successes. How we handle each is what He is interested in. After all, He is the one that has given us the talents we have and the opportunities to succeed. No matter what you believe, I hope you can agree that certain people and circumstances are brought into our lives for a reason. We may not know what those reasons are but I am not sure we are always supposed to know. It is important to always be ready to be a playmaker.

If we see the finish line in sight and choose to jog or slow down then we are resting on our accomplishments. We are surrendering all of the passion we had, the passion that got us to this point, and making a choice to coast the rest of the way. Proverbs tells us, do not be sluggish because if you are you will not be able to reap the rewards that you have worked so hard to attain. On the other hand, if we continue to give our best and be diligent to the end then our prize will be waiting for us when we cross the finish line.

So where is the finish line? I cannot answer that for you, because I do not know. We may have many finish lines in life or maybe we just have one. Sometimes I think that we have many situations that are brought upon us, like tests, and God is watching closely to see how we run that particular race. Other times I think we have only one finish line and that line comes when we are physically no longer a part of this world, when we meet God and pass through the gates of heaven. No matter how many races there are, I know that God is watching to see how we run the race (remember the verse I mentioned in chapter 2, 1 Corinthians 9:24).

We should wake up each day, feel blessed to have another chance to be a little different and use our platform the way it was intended to be used. Give thanks for the ability to compete, impact other individuals, and let our light shine. The finish line will be revealed to us when we are supposed to know where it is. Until then, we have to keep living our life with passion, diligence and with a purpose to be better today than we were yesterday. If we can do that then we will choose to sprint though the finish line with every ounce of fuel we have in our tanks. We will not walk briskly (because if you do I will have to start speaking loudly again).

Parents, Coaches Mentors….Last Thought

In previous chapters I have reserved this section of the book to talk about things I see we, as mentors or parents, could do in order to help those we influence to become better. In this chapter I want to express a few parting thoughts and say, "Thank you."

When I set out to write this book I wanted to accomplish one thing. I wanted to help people improve their lives. I work in athletics and see examples every day of the progress that we could all make if we just had a roadmap to follow. I am not saying that I have the exact formula to ensure that everyone who is athletic or competes finds success. But I have presented many principles that we could all incorporate into our lives to see improvements. If this book sparked discussions on any level, then the book accomplished its mission. You, as parents or mentors, have the tough task of being loving role models, disciplinarians and motivators. I want to thank you for taking the time to read this book. I hope something you read caught your attention enough to initiate changes or deeper conversations that you have not had before.

When my sister Sarah passed away, I made it my goal to do something positive. I wanted to develop something that could be presented to groups or individuals and offer a change in people's lives for the better. I have spent hours talking with my family on what we, as a family, could do to impact people, especially youth, in a positive way. This book is a result of all of those conversations. I am fortunate to have parents that exemplify selfless love and are great leaders. Speaking of great leaders, I want to leave you with one last Tim Tebow story from the video I watched.

Tim was talking about what it meant to him to finish strong. He talked about how, on the field during practice, he would urge his teammates to run just a few more sprints. He told how in the weight room the team would motivate each other to do just one more set, to not give up but rather to give just a little more. During his junior year, when his team won the national championship, his team's motto of finishing strong was put to the test. In the championship game the Gators found themselves down in the second half but with the football. He explained that he and his teammates huddled and talked about how this was their chance to finish the game, to finish strong, just as they had all season long in their preparation leading up to this moment. To make a long story a little shorter, they went down the field and scored to take the lead and win the game. When Tim walked to the sideline something happened that Tim referred to as one of the greatest joys he has had. Tim walked to his coach, Urban Meyer, who took off his headset, gave Tim a hug, patted him on the back and said, "Hey Timmy, you finished. That-a-boy, great job." Tim explained that, to him, there was no better feeling as an athlete than to have his coach pat him on the back and say, "That-a-boy," and congratulate him for finishing strong. All of the hard work that he had put in up to that point had paid off. But do you know what Tim's ultimate goal is? He explained that his ultimate goal would be fulfilled when he dies and is standing before Jesus Christ. That Jesus Christ will walk up to him, take off his headset and say, "Hey Timmy, great job, you finished. That-a-boy, that-a-boy."

I know as parents and mentors you have a difficult job in front of you, but it is not impossible. If we influence those around us to work hard, compete for the right reasons, give glory where it is deserved, use their platform to be a positive influence, dare to be different though passion and their belief in themselves, to give their very best and become a playmaker then, one day when we see that finish line before us, we will know what to do. We will sprint and become a little more diligent in our goal to cross that line while going as fast as our fuel will allow. When we do cross that line, Jesus Christ will be waiting for us. He will pull off his headset and say, "Great race, I am glad you decided to run. Way to finish strong. Great job, I am proud of you."

Made in the USA
Charleston, SC
18 February 2014